Also available at all good book stores

9781785317927

9781801500630

9781801500067

9781785318627

9781801500906

9781905411832

9781785318641

9781785313318

9781785315459

SCOTLAND'S
SWEDISH ADVENTURE

John Bleasdale

SCOTLAND'S
SWEDISH ADVENTURE

*The Story of
Scotland's European
Championship Debut*

First published by Pitch Publishing, 2022

Pitch Publishing
9 Donnington Park,
85 Birdham Road,
Chichester,
West Sussex,
PO20 7AJ
www.pitchpublishing.co.uk
info@pitchpublishing.co.uk

A CIP catalogue record is available for this book
from the British Library.

ISBN 978 1 80150 110 1

Typesetting and origination by Pitch Publishing
Printed and bound in India by Replika Press Pvt. Ltd.

Contents

I would like to dedicate this book to my two wonderful sons, Callum and Henry. I hope they can be proud of me when they look at this book.

I would also like to dedicate this book to the memory of my grandfather Robert McNee. This is for you, Granda.

Foreword by Craig Brown

HAVING HAD the good fortune to be on the SFA staff at three FIFA World Cup finals tournaments and two UEFA Championship finals, arguably the Euro '92 European Championship in Sweden was the most significant. The reason for this assertion is that it was the first time Scotland had qualified for the Euros. The latest involvement was the third, Euro '96 being sandwiched between '92 and 2021.

It should be remembered that it was far more difficult to get to the finals as then only eight teams competed. So great credit is due to Andy Roxburgh for having us among the elite of Europe and have Scotland officially placed fifth in the tournament. I was Andy's assistant and was privileged to see the work he put in and the manner in which it was reciprocated by the grateful players. Grateful? Yes, of course, because every professional footballer will testify to the fact that the highlight of his playing career is representing his country in the finals stage of the World Cup or European Championship.

In this superb and insightful Euro '92 chronicle of events, John Bleasdale's observations resonate fully with my own memories. There is no doubt in my mind that two things dominate my recollections. Firstly, that we were desperately unfortunate not to progress further and, secondly, the response from the fans was wonderful.

We emerged from a difficult series of group games against Switzerland, Romania, San Marino and Bulgaria with only one defeat, inflicted by a single Gheorghe Hagi penalty for Romania. Our talisman in the early qualification games was John Robertson, who scored vital goals against Romania and Switzerland. The irony of Robbo's success was that he ended up missing the finals through injury, which was a double blow for him given that, along with Davie Cooper, he was unfit to join the World Cup squad for Italy two years previously.

It was the case that at the three FIFA World Cups for which we qualified, on each occasion Scotland had to go without their best player. It was Kenny Dalglish for Alex Ferguson's squad in Mexico '86, Cooper and Robertson for Andy Roxburgh's Italia '90 group and Gary McAllister for my time with the team in

France '98. There was no such missing superstar for the European Championship in Sweden '92.

Any fair-minded independent observer would surely concede that Scotland were desperately unlucky in Sweden. In an even game against the defending champions, the Dutch with world-class exponents such as Van Basten, Gullit, Wouters and Rijkaard, it took a typical piece of brilliance by Dennis Bergkamp to inflict a 0-1 defeat on us.

But for the brilliance of Illgner, the German goalkeeper, we would have emerged with at least something from the second match, but again we conceded when Effenberg's shot was deflected past Andy Goram by Maurice Malpas. This second goal, added to Riedle's first-half strike, inflicted on us another unfortunate defeat; although, again, I felt we played in a creditable manner against the world champions.

Our final match in Sweden resulted in a resounding victory over the former USSR, now changed their name to the CIS. A brilliant shot from Paul McStay, a long-range attempt from Brian McClair and a fine penalty from Gary McAllister when Pat Nevin was fouled gave us a pleasing 3-0 win, much to the delight of the tremendously loyal Tartan Army who stayed behind to acknowledge the gargantuan efforts of the lads.

No major competition can be reported without mention of the famous, yes genuinely famous, Tartan Army. My experience of 15 years travelling extensively with the best fans in the world confirms my bold assertion. In 1992 the customary good nature and resourcefulness was abundantly apparent. With the demand for, and cost of, hotel rooms, many of the supporters had the initiative to make their temporary living accommodation in tents. On the way to training one morning our team coach drove past a large field of tents about twice the size of a football pitch. On seeing this marvellous sight, with banners and flags draped over the tents, thoughtful Andy Roxburgh asked the driver to drive the team coach into the field. To see hundreds of fans awakening from their sleep and crawling out of their tents and making for the coach was like looking at an enlarged anthill.

In his customary eloquent manner, Andy thanked everyone for the wonderful support, and the players patiently and willingly posed for photographs and signed literally hundreds of autographs. The goodwill was indeed tangible! One game out of three had been won yet the backing was overwhelmingly positive. That, then, describes the mantra of the renowned Tartan Army.

There's an emotive introduction to a book on South American football, *Soccer in Sun and Shadow*, written by Eduardo Galeano. The four short lines accurately sum up the feelings of our Euro '92 players and staff, together with the Scotland supporters in Sweden:

We lost
We won
Either way
We had fun.

We did, yet again, in Sweden '92!

Introduction

Friday, 12 June 1992 at the Ullevi Stadium, Gothenburg

HISTORY FOR the Scotland men's national team was made as they made their debut at the European Championship finals in Sweden. Despite qualifying for each of the previous five World Cup finals between 1974 and 1990, the talents of Dalglish, Bremner, Souness, Robertson and co. never once got close to helping their country qualify for the Euros.

It didn't help that there were fewer Euros slots available back in the 70s, which was just a four-team tournament, and 80s, which expanded to eight teams, compared to the World Cup containing ten and then 14 UEFA nations in its 16- and 24-team tournaments respectively. It was also well-documented that the priority during those European Championship qualifying campaigns was to rebuild for the next World Cup qualifying campaign, and ensure we got to the world's biggest stage.

That focussed changed in 1990 under manager Andy Roxburgh.

Appointed after the Mexico '86 World Cup, Roxburgh's appointment was not met with approval amongst many of the media and the Tartan Army, with cries of 'Andy who?' being echoed across the country. If that wasn't hard enough, Roxburgh was following on from the late Jock Stein, who'd sadly died under a year earlier, and Sir Alex Ferguson, who oversaw the Mexico adventure before deciding against staying on with the national team.

Things didn't get off to the best start under his tenure as Scotland failed to reach the Euro '88 finals, finishing a distant fourth in their qualifying group, behind Republic of Ireland, Bulgaria and Belgium. However, like his predecessors, he was given the next World Cup qualifying campaign, and things were on the up as Scotland qualified for Italia '90 ahead of a France side containing the talents of Jean-Pierre Papin and Eric Cantona. Unfortunately, defeat to Costa Rica, and another early exit, put Roxburgh on the back foot once again, and this heightened the need to reach Sweden even further.

Overcoming those hurdles makes it even more impressive that Andy Roxburgh managed to guide Scotland to the European Championship, becoming the first men's national team manager to do so. They also came through a very tough group to get to Sweden by overcoming Romania, Switzerland and Bulgaria, who would all go on to perform admirably at the USA '94 World Cup and, collectively, had star names like Gheorghe Hagi, Stephane Chapuisat and Hristo Stoichkov amongst their ranks. Being one of just eight European nations out of a possible 33 to get to these finals was a major achievement, and one that is grossly underappreciated by many observers when looking back at their favourite tournament watching the men's national team. Nowadays, of course, you have 55 nations trying to qualify for a 24-team European Championship, which shows how much the landscape of Europe has changed in the last three decades.

The finals themselves threw Scotland in the most difficult draw imaginable. First up would be the defending European Champions, the Netherlands, followed by a meeting with the reigning World Champions, Germany, before concluding their campaign against the CIS, formerly known as the Soviet Union, who had reached the Euro '88 Final. Despite the obvious quality they were up against, Roxburgh and his players stood firm and went toe-to-toe with their superior rivals, and created numerous chances along the way. Whilst the records show we lost the opening two games that saw us go out of the tournament, there were plenty of plaudits for the way the team performed against the Dutch and Germans respectively, with a resounding win over the CIS giving Scotland a fitting farewell.

Then there's the small matter of the Tartan Army. Their reputation soared in Sweden for their exemplary behaviour, which was in stark contrast to the hooligan element that tarnished the reputation of England supporters at Euro '92, and it led to an unprecedented UEFA Fair Play Award. Roxburgh also ensured that his players appreciated their following by taking them to visit supporters at a nearby campsite in between matches, and by arranging a post-match photograph with the Tartan Army in the background after the final game.

In many ways, Scotland's Euro '92 campaign doesn't get the recognition it deserves. Ultimately, we went out in the first round, the same as every other major international finals, but there is an argument that this was our best performance, in terms of who we were up against and the chances we created against some of the best players on the continent. In the final standings, Scotland were, statistically, the fifth-best side in the competition, which is a pretty decent accomplishment compared to the other finals we've been to, yet people generally don't recall this as fondly as frustrating World Cup campaigns or Euro '96.

Scotland's Swedish Adventure tells the story of those who were involved in that historic campaign. From the management team of Andy Roxburgh and Craig Brown to the players, from those in the media to the fans, there's many a great tale to tell about Scotland's European Championship debut in Sweden back in 1992.

But before we get to Gothenburg and Norrkoping, let's go back to where the journey began – a wet Wednesday evening in September 1990 at Hampden Park.

Recovery from apathy

SCOTLAND'S JOURNEY to Sweden wasn't exactly plain sailing. There were some difficult obstacles to overcome throughout their qualification campaign in their bid to achieve something that arguably greater Scotland men's national sides couldn't do before.

In fact, right back at the very start of this campaign, not all was rosy in the Scotland camp going into the opening game against top seeds Romania at Hampden. The report card from Italia '90 did not make for great reading amongst most critics. Sure, the records will say that Scotland exited the World Cup on goal difference for the fourth time in five tournaments. They will also point out that it took a combination of a Jim Leighton error and a world-class save by Taffarel from Mo Johnston that saw us go down 1-0 to Brazil in a game where a draw would've taken us through to the knockout stages.

However, the disappointing result in the opening game against Costa Rica was, undoubtedly, our downfall and, despite an impressive performance and result against Sweden in the second game, it became too big a task to recover. Add to that reports of player unrest in the camp, there was an air of apathy towards the men's national team going into the Euro '92 qualifying campaign.

Journalist Hugh MacDonald, who was still going to matches as a fan back then before his successful career in the newspaper industry, remembers the negative atmosphere towards the Scotland side following Italia '90, and that Roxburgh was very much a man under scrutiny at that time. He said: 'There was a lot of disillusion after the World Cup. It's quite funny when you look back in the cold light of day, our record in World Cups is pretty decent in the group stages. You would take it now. Costa Rica, for example, doesn't look such a bad result in hindsight as it did at the time, but at the time it was a dreadful result. Every time, it was portrayed as a sort of republic that no one had ever heard of, it was almost a humiliating result. So yeah, there was a lot of apathy. And remember as well, by 1991/92, we had a wee bit of history of qualifying for World Cups as well, so the ache of never qualifying for anything had passed, possibly to be replaced by a bit of disillusion once we got to finals.'

It summed up the level of expectation, that Scotland came under fire after that tournament; after all, it was their fifth consecutive appearance at a World Cup finals. Guiding the team to Italy in the first place definitely helped buy Roxburgh more time in the job, though it was not too uncommon in those days for international managers to get more than two campaigns, as demonstrated with two of his predecessors, Willie Ormond and Jock Stein. Even Ally MacLeod, for all the ridicule he was subjected to after Argentina '78, was given the following European Championship qualifying campaign before he tendered his resignation after the opening qualifier against Austria.

Each of those subsequent European Championship qualifying attempts would end in disappointment as Scotland would often finish a distant third or fourth in their section. Despite this, there were no calls for managers' heads as it was clear that Scotland were building for the next round of World Cup qualifiers, which, as discussed in the introduction, had greater odds of qualification.

That mentality would change after Italy, and Roxburgh made it his mission to become the first manager of the Scotland men's national team to lead his side to a European Championship finals. He revealed that his bosses at the SFA shared this vision and made qualification to the finals in Sweden their immediate priority over building for the next World Cup in the USA. In an interview we conducted for *Famous Tartan Army Magazine*, Roxburgh said: 'All I was asked to do was get us to the next World Cup, and then when we got to that World Cup once that task was completed, it was one of these things – "Well, why don't we try to get to the Euros? We've never done that before so why don't we add that on." And that became the next challenge. It flowed from one thing on to the other, that's the background to it.'

A total of 34 UEFA nations were entered for the 1992 European Championship qualification draw, which was made in February 1990. The initial format would see six groups containing five nations and one group of just four, where only the side finishing top of the section would join hosts Sweden at the finals. This quickly changed when West and East Germany, coincidentally drawn together in the same group, unified that year, resulting in just one German side competing in international competition going forward, making it 33 nations fighting for just seven spots in the tournament.

Little did we know it at the time, the German reunification would begin the change of the European landscape, and in their case the amalgamation of two nations or states would be an exception. By the time the draw for the finals came around, the Soviet Union would break up and ten new nations would be formed as a result. Shortly before the finals themselves, Yugoslavia were forced to withdraw from the tournament amidst the ongoing war that saw Croatia, Slovenia, Macedonia and Bosnia Herzegovina become independent, whilst Czechoslovakia broke up in 1993 to become Slovakia and the Czech Republic. By the time the qualifying draw for the 1996 edition of the European Championship came around in January 1994, there were 46 UEFA nations taking part for 15 available spaces alongside hosts England (the 48th UEFA nation, Yugoslavia, were still banned from international competition following their political issues). Nowadays, the Euros has increased to 24 teams as there are now 55 UEFA nations, where the delayed Euro 2020 finals saw qualification spots for the top two sides and winners from the inaugural UEFA Nations League for the multi-host competition. It really is changed days!

Back onto the Euro '92 qualifying draw, there would be no second chances for the sides who finished runners-up or even the safety net of a play-off via the Nations League in the current climate. Only the seven group winners would qualify for the finals, so it was first or nowhere! Scotland were given pot two status and the draw saw them placed in Group 2, alongside top seeds Romania, a Bulgaria side from pot three whom they'd beaten in Euro '88 qualification to deny them a place in West Germany, pot four side Switzerland, and minnows San Marino from pot five, who were making their debut in international-competition history.

It could be argued that Romania were the preferred option from pot one when you consider the other possibilities we could've got. The other top-seeded sides were reigning European Champions the Netherlands, newly crowned World Champions West Germany (latterly becoming Germany as previously highlighted), World Cup semi-finalists Italy and England, quarter-finalists at Italia '90 Yugoslavia, and a tough Spain side. On paper, the Romanians were less daunting, but they were a more-than-capable side, as they showed in Italy when they defeated the Soviet Union and drew with Argentina en route to the last 16, where only a penalty shoot-out saw them exit the finals to Republic of Ireland. They had the talents of Gheorghe Hagi, who had moved to Real Madrid that summer and would also go on to play for Barcelona, which gives an indication of what a top player he was. Add to that the goalscoring threat of Marius Lacatus and Florin Raducioiu, plus future Chelsea full-back Dan Petrescu, and you get the idea of the quality the Romanians possessed.

Hagi and co. rolled into Glasgow for the opening night of Euro '92 qualification on Wednesday, 12 September 1990, confident that they could come away from Hampden with a positive start. Scotland, on the other hand, had to overcome their post-Italia '90 blues if they were going to get off to a winning start in their bid to reach their first-ever European Championship finals. Interestingly, it was two points for a victory at this point and not the three you see more commonly in the modern era. Another key rule back in the Euro '92 adventure was that goalkeepers could still pick up back passes passed by foot, with the change not being implemented until after the finals in Sweden.

It may have been billed as a crucial match prior to kick-off, but it didn't convince the general public as a paltry crowd of just 12,801 entered the national stadium. Stuart McCall may have missed the game through injury, but he was all too aware of the apathy surrounding the men's national team going into that opening game and the effect it had on the crowd. Having played in all three games at Italia '90, and netting his solitary Scotland goal to open the scoring in the 2-1 victory over Sweden, he admits to being a little puzzled at how much the post-Italia '90 hangover affected the nation. 'I remember the crowd not being big,' he said, 'but when I look back and there was only 12,800 there, that shows you the apathy that was surrounding it. I even thought, having been involved in the World Cup, that we let the nation down against Costa Rica, but then I thought we won them over with the performance against Sweden, and certainly the performance against Brazil where we were unfortunate not to go through. I don't know why there was such apathy, I've got to be honest. Everyone will remember the Costa Rica game, but I don't think we came home in disgrace because we won the Sweden game and pushed Brazil all the way.'

Whilst apathy played its part, there were other factors behind the low attendance that wet Wednesday evening. Despite what fans growing up in the modern era might think, the midweek slot was not one of them as almost all qualifying matches for international competitions were played in midweek, with weekend games not becoming a thing until the mid- to late-90s. Wednesday night games were most definitely the norm for international football in 1990.

What was rare was that the game was broadcast live on BBC One Scotland. The television contract allowed just one home qualifier to be screened live to the nation, along with all away matches, with the rest of the home games being restricted to highlights only. They decided on this game, with it being against the top-seeded side in the group, and the game being televised was also considered a factor behind the low turnout. Ronnie McDevitt, Tartan Army foot soldier and author of four books focussed on the Scotland national team, including *A Life in The Tartan Army*, summed all of this up by saying: 'The World Cup in Italy had disappointed a lot of Scotland fans, and although the Sweden game had been memorable, there was still disbelief and a feeling the staff and players had let us down over the Costa Rica fiasco. No one saw that coming and it left supporters feeling angry, and a lot were considering calling time on the national side after yet another failure to reach round two. The build-up had also been less than inspiring, and a win over Argentina was soon forgotten about following home defeats to Egypt and East Germany, and an awful, lacklustre draw with Poland in Glasgow.

'This apathy was reflected in the attendance for the Romania game at Hampden, our first match since Italy. However, this figure deserves greater inspection as it is often overlooked that the match was shown live on BBC One. BBC Scotland's agreement for exclusive rights to cover the European qualifiers were a package of highlights for all the home games and live screenings of the away fixtures. They also managed to secure permission to show one of the home games of the broadcaster's choice live and the opener was selected. It was in fact the first time a European

Championship qualifier at home had been allowed live coverage by the SFA.'

Fellow foot soldier Kevin Donnelly added in a third factor behind the low attendance – that the SFA admitted putting the ticket prices too high. He said: 'I know Marjorie Nimmo, who used to run the Travel Club, and she said it was all to do with the pricing for that game. She said they got the pricing totally wrong. I was working in London at the time, so I went to very few games, but you've got to remember there were no cheap flights; you couldn't go up on a Wednesday afternoon and back down on a Thursday morning and only take one day's leave.'

All of that was very much secondary to Roxburgh's problems as his concern was putting out a side capable of beating the Romanians to collect maximum points. His cause wasn't helped by the loss of experienced pros Roy Aitken (who captained the side in Italy), Maurice Johnston and Jim Bett who, for various reasons, were no longer available for selection. Bett and Johnston had retired from international football, whilst Aitken, although he didn't formally retire, told Roxburgh that he wanted to take a step back to focus on the remainder of his club career, where he was at Newcastle United at the time, and spending time with his family. Johnston and Aitken would both come out of their hiatus at some point later in the campaign, whereas Bett never played for his country again.

A surprise inclusion in the squad was Jim Leighton, who was selected along with Andy Goram and Campbell Money as one of the three goalkeepers Roxburgh picked in his 21-man squad. It was particularly surprising given that he was now well out of the picture at Manchester United after being dropped for the 1990 FA Cup Final replay against Crystal Palace. In addition, he was heavily criticised for his role in Brazil's late winner in Turin by fumbling Alemao's shot back into a dangerous area where, after a scramble involving Alex McLeish, Careca and himself, Muller tapped in the goal that sent Scotland home before the postcards – again!

This would be the only time that Leighton would be called up during Scotland's European Championship adventure, and he didn't even make the substitutes' bench. Throughout our quest to reach the Euros, Leighton went on to have mixed spells at Reading, Arsenal and Dundee, and wasn't even considered for a call-up for any further internationals during this period. It was only when he joined Hibernian in 1993 that he regained his form consistently enough to earn a Scotland recall, long after Euro '92 was over.

Filling Leighton's position between the sticks was an easy one. Andy Goram had been deputy to

Leighton since the 1986 World Cup in Mexico – now it was his chance to show that he could handle the pressure of being the Scotland number one. Even though his club side, Hibernian, were struggling in the Scottish Premier Division that season, Roxburgh had enough trust that the man nicknamed 'the Goalie' was good enough to make the step up and showcase his goalkeeping abilities on the international stage. Not only did Goram make the position his own but his performances for club and country earned him a move to Rangers the following summer to take over from then-England number one Chris Woods, who'd gone to Sheffield Wednesday.

In front of Goram, there was a space needing to be filled alongside Alex McLeish at centre-back, caused by injuries to Richard Gough, Dave McPherson and Craig Levein, along with the retirement of Willie Miller, who never recovered from the serious knee injury sustained against Norway. Brian Irvine had stepped into Miller's shoes at Aberdeen and won many plaudits for his performances. Now he was asked to do the same for his country by forming a partnership with McLeish in the centre of defence.

Irvine must've thought he was living in a fairy tale in 1990, first scoring the winning penalty for Aberdeen in the Scottish Cup Final and now being picked to play for his country in a crucial qualifying match at Hampden. In an interview conducted for Scottish Football Forums Podcast in April 2020, Irvine reflected on the honour of being picked for Scotland and playing a small part in this story with his performance. He said: 'I was always a football supporter who got a chance to be a professional footballer player, so winning the Scottish Cup and the League Cup as well is about as joyful as can be. Beyond that level with Scotland, it's a new level; everyone dreams about playing for their country, and when I got the opportunity to play for Scotland it was "pinch me" stuff. And in such an important game, because it was the opening game of the European Championship qualifiers against Romania, who were a good team, and we got a good win. I was just picked to play alongside Alex McLeish and Stewart McKimmie with the Aberdeen connection, and that helped me settle into the game, and thankfully we managed to get a win against Romania and eventually qualified for Sweden. I didn't play in any other games, but I remember Andy Roxburgh always saying on a television programme once, thanking me for coming into the squad and playing my part, and I'm glad that I played a small part in the '92 success of Scotland qualifying for Sweden.'

With Stewart McKimmie and Maurice Malpas in both full-back positions, the back four was made up entirely of players from the New Firm clubs. A fourth Aberdeen player, Robert Connor, also came in for a surprise start to line up in a midfield that contained Gary McAllister, captain for the night Paul McStay, and Murdo MacLeod, who, like Irvine, was not selected for the initial squad but was drafted in as a result of McCall's injury. Whilst there was no natural width in that midfield, it wasn't short in creativity and would be an indicator of how Scotland would look to play throughout the course of their Euro '92 adventure.

Although the midfield had a creative look to it, the players across the middle of the park were all too aware of their defensive responsibilities as well, particularly with Gheorghe Hagi to try and contain. Connor was in awe of Hagi's abilities, revealing in an interview with Scottish Football Forums Podcast in October 2020 that he considered Hagi the toughest opponent in his career. He said: 'The Romania game was memorable for two things. One being that we won the game, the other being was that I played directly against the best player I've ever seen live, which was Gheorghe Hagi. Unfortunately, he was playing directly against me so I got a really good view of him, not that I got that close to him! The guy was fantastic and he was probably, at that time, one of the top three best players in the world. They also had another top player, Lacatus, and a few other really good players at Romania, who were a right good side at that time, but playing against Hagi tells you something about just how far away these players are from just a normal player like me. This guy was different class, just seeing things that nobody else could see, and [it was] just a kind of education watching this guy play. Having said that, it was great to win the game.'

Up front, Ally McCoist was partnered by debutant John Robertson. It was a long-awaited debut for Robbo, who had been scoring goals for fun at Hearts for a few seasons but was often overlooked due to the form of Johnston and the performances of others playing in England and abroad, like Gordon Durie, Alan McInally, Robert Fleck and Brian McClair. Despite having no caps, he was set to go to the World Cup, before injury deprived him of the chance to go to Italy. However, a combination of a good start to the season, Johnston's retirement and injuries to McClair and McInally provided Robertson with his chance to prove to Roxburgh and his assistant Craig Brown that he could carry that goal threat on to the international scene and justify why they were keen to take him to Italia '90 in the first place.

Robertson had been given extra motivation going into the game thanks to an unwanted phone call from his club chairman, Wallace Mercer, to Andy Roxburgh. Unhappy that his striker criticised his decision to sack Alex MacDonald as Hearts manager, Mercer phoned Roxburgh demanding that Robertson be sent home from the squad. Luckily, as Robertson revealed in his autobiography *Robbo: My Autobiography*, Mercer's intervention had the opposite effect as Roxburgh decided to start him.

He said:'He said: 'The morning of the Romanian match saw us take a leisurely walk by the famous Troon Golf Course and, as we headed back for lunch, I was told to go and see Andy Roxburgh. He informed me he had received a call from Wallace Mercer asking me to be sent back to Edinburgh immediately as, given my comments on the gaffers sacking, I was obviously in no fit state to play mentally. Andy looked at me and said "John, up until this morning, I wasn't sure if I was going to play you or not but, given your admiration for Alex and then hearing that Wallace wants you back now, I have a feeling that with that fire in your belly you will do well tonight, so I am starting you up front with Ally." I assured him I was ready to give everything and after lunch the team was named and I was to get my first cap at Hampden.'

Scotland team: Goram, McKimmie, Malpas, McAllister (Nevin 73), McLeish, Irvine, Robertson, McStay, McCoist, MacLeod, Connor (Boyd 59)

So a Scotland side dealing with apathy, the embarrassment of a low crowd and huge disruption to its regular starting XI took to the field on a rainy night at Hampden to face the top seeds in the group. That apathy looked as though it would continue as the Romanians began brightly and took the lead after just 13 minutes when Rodion Camataru tapped home from close range after Dan Petrescu's mishit shot.

But Scotland galvanised and could've been level when Malpas played the ball to McCoist down the left-hand channel. The striker cut past a defender on to his right foot, but he dragged his effort past goalkeeper Silviu Lung's right-hand post. As Scotland strived to get back into the game, the visitors remained a threat on the counter-attack and could easily have doubled their advantage when Camataru's cross looped over McLeish's head into the path of Marius Lacatus, but his first-time volley lacked conviction and went straight into the grateful arms of Andy Goram.

After surviving that scare, the hosts then got themselves back on level terms after 37 minutes. McKimmie ran with the ball into the area and teed up McAllister on the edge of the box. He then clipped the ball high into the penalty area for McCoist to outjump his marker and nod it down for Robertson to prod home from around six yards. It was the dream debut for Robbo to mark it with a goal. More importantly, it gave Scotland the boost they needed going into the half-time break.

Recalling that moment in his autobiography and what it meant in terms of the context of the game, Robbo said: 'Stewart McKimmie floated in a cros from the left, Coisty went up for it and he managed to outjump the centre-half. I did as I was taught, gambled on him winning it and got the sole of my boot ahead of Popescu to stab it home. We were level and I had scored on my debut. This seemed to knock the stuffing out of the Romanians and we picked up in the second half and got about them as the small crowd suddenly sensed we had a real chance.'

Into the second half, and Romania began as brightly as they started the first by taking the game to the Scots. They looked as though they were about to take the lead when Lacatus's pass found Petrescu inside the penalty area. He managed to sidestep McLeish and was about to pull the trigger when Irvine came across to bail out his centre-back partner with a terrific slide tackle and the ball trickled harmlessly into Goram's hands. The Goalie's services were required a few minutes later, when Hagi hit a free kick from the left-hand corner of the penalty area, but he was equal to Hagi's powerful shot to push the ball away to safety.

From there, Scotland began to assert themselves on the top-seeded side and very nearly took the lead past the hour mark. Robertson's cross from the left-hand side was brilliantly controlled by McCoist. He then faked to shoot, stepped inside Michael Klein, but his left-foot shot was brilliantly saved by the left foot of Lung and wide of the post. Following the resultant corner, McCoist crossed the ball back into the area for an unmarked Gary McAllister, but his first-time volley was weak and easily gathered by the Romanian goalkeeper and captain. McAllister would make Lung work harder with his next effort, a low shot from an indirect free kick set up by Murdo MacLeod. The big keeper had to get down low to parry the shot, then get up quickly as McCoist pounced on the rebound, but he was flagged for offside.

Sensing that his side had the Romanians on the ropes at this point, Roxburgh made use of the two substitutions he was allowed in that era as Scotland chased the winner to gain the crucial two points. He brought on Motherwell captain and utility man Tom Boyd, another player drafted in due to the withdrawal of an injured player (in this case, Steve Nicol) for his international debut, and Everton winger Pat Nevin, gambling that their pace would pin the Romanians back. It paid off on 75 minutes as Boyd went on a sauntering run down the left-hand side. He then played the ball back to Robertson where he and McStay worked it to Murdo MacLeod on the right.

MacLeod hit the ball across the face of goal, where Ally McCoist got in front of his marker to knock home from a couple of yards. Scotland saw out the last quarter of an hour to hold on for victory.

It may only have been the first game, but this was a crucial win for the Scots against the group favourites. All the apathy clamoured at the men's national team before the game was almost forgotten about. Now there was hope that Scotland could do something in this group. Even if he was playing it down, there's no doubt that the pre-match negativity was playing on Andy Roxburgh's mind, and for him to still put a team out on the park capable of defeating a pot one team says a lot about his managerial skills that often didn't get the credit they deserved.

Reflecting on the event, Roxburgh said: 'When you're restarting after a finals like that, I think there's always an element of people thinking, "Let's wait and see what happens." After the World Cup, there was a kind of lull, if you like, and it was up to us and to the team to build up the expectations again. At the time, Romania wasn't viewed as a big draw. I think had we been playing Germany in the opening qualifying round, you'd maybe have a big crowd. Then into the bargain, in the build-up to that opening game, we had a whole lot of injuries. We had a series of injury problems, so I think the whole combination of elements came together. It wasn't a great turnout from a Scottish perspective, but our attitude was [that] we had to prove ourselves again; that's what you've always got to do in football is prove yourself again, so our job there was to make sure we got off to a good start and, fortunately, despite all the injury problems, we did get off to a good start.'

From a player's perspective, it would've been a culture shock seeing Hampden at less than half capacity as they walked out onto the pitch to see more empty spaces in the terracing than Saltire and Lion Rampant flags. Maurice Malpas had played in many big occasions for club and country at the national stadium, so he was as surprised as any by the low turnout, but he and the team had to put that to one side to get the result.

Malpas said: 'It was a bit of a shock because I was used to playing in front of a full house just about every game I played. It's just one of those things. You've got to adapt as a player and get on with it. We had to make sure we picked up some points at home, and that was the case.'

A little over a month later, it was the turn of pot-four side Switzerland to come to Hampden. Despite their pot four status, the Swiss were no mugs and definitely one of the strongest sides from this section. They also possessed a promising side, with the talents of Alain Sutter in midfield and a lethal strike force in Adrian Knup, Stephane Chapuisat and Kubilay Turkyilmaz, and they laid down their intentions with a 2-0 home win over Bulgaria in the opening game.

Four changes were made to the Scotland side from the one that defeated Romania. Dave McPherson returned to the starting line-up in place of Brian Irvine, Stuart McCall replaced the injured McStay, and Boyd was rewarded for his impact against the Romanians with a first start for his country, replacing Robert Connor.

Although named in this squad, Irvine and Connor would not be used again in this campaign, whilst their club team-mate Alex McLeish was given the captain's armband for this game.

The fourth change saw Steve Nicol come in for the injured Malpas at left-back. Nicol was omitted from the original squad as Roxburgh stood against what was deemed, according to the *Glasgow Herald*, a cavalier attitude by Nicol's club side Liverpool, which resulted in Nicol withdrawing from the Romania game without a medical certificate. The standoff was ended when Roxburgh received a letter of apology from the Liverpool chief executive, Peter Robinson, and Nicol answered his country's call for this crucial game. Liverpool manager and Scotland legend Kenny

Dalglish was also quoted as saying that this oversight would not happen again.

> Scotland team: Goram, McKimmie, Nicol, McCall, McPherson, McLeish, Robertson, McAllister (Collins 79), McCoist, MacLeod, Boyd (Durie 68)

It was a much-improved attendance inside the national stadium as 27,740 fans came along to see if the Scots could build on that opening victory. They had a golden opportunity midway through the first half when McCoist was cleaned out by goalkeeper Philipp Walker as the striker attempted to go round him. Referee Esa Antero Palso had no hesitation in pointing to the spot, and there were few protestations from the Swiss. Hampden was then stunned as McCoist pulled his penalty wide of the post, and the visitors breathed a sigh of relief.

The deadlock was finally broken on 34 minutes after referee Palso spotted a handball in the penalty area by Swiss defender Andre Egli, which their manager, Uwe Stielike, hotly contested. Unnerved by the delays caused by the Swiss protests, John Robertson stepped up to send Walker the wrong way and put Scotland ahead with his second goal in as many games for his country.

Seven minutes into the second half, and the lead was doubled when McCall headed a loose ball forward into the path of Gary McAllister, who then set himself to unleash a right-footed half-volley towards goal. Although Walker got a hand to it, the shot was too powerful to keep out and McAllister, who was now establishing himself in the Scotland side, scored his first international goal. It was a memorable moment for the midfielder, who was now really making a name for himself after joining Leeds United in the summer, where he would go on to win a league title prior to the Euro '92 finals.

McCall, though, has little recollection of his role in the goal, so much so that he'd actually forgotten that it was he who headed the ball through for McAllister to lash home. When 'recalling' that moment, he said, 'Somebody said to me, "Did you play in that game?" And I went, "I know I remember missing the first one, but I'm sure I played in both games against Switzerland." Then I clicked on it and watched the goal, had to rewind it and thought, "Was that me?" Because I had forgot it was me who headed it through. I can remember most things but I genuinely did! A memorable assist, which I forgot about. But I remember Gaz Mac smashing it across and smashing it in.'

You would've thought that Scotland were on easy street, but as most Scots fans know, that term doesn't exist. The Swiss got back into the game on 65 minutes, when Turkyilmaz was adjudged to have been pulled down by McLeish. It looked soft, but the Finnish official chose to give the third penalty kick of the evening, and Knup successfully despatched it into the bottom right-hand corner, despite Goram's best efforts to keep it out. The complexion of the game changed as Scotland dropped deeper, in hope of defending their now-slender lead, while the Swiss chased the equaliser they craved, and they should've had one with just a few minutes left. Alain Sutter crossed from the right-hand side, Knup flicked it on to an unmarked Turkyilmaz, who'd ghosted in unnoticed at the back post and somehow, from around four yards, scooped the ball over the bar.

The Swiss' misery was compounded with two minutes to go when they were reduced to ten men after Egli body-checked Gordon Durie, who was attempting to run past him. Scotland managed to hang on and take the two points. Stielike had to be held back by his assistants to prevent him running up to referee Palso. The Tartan Army weren't caring as they went home delighted with what turned out to be a crucial victory. McCall had better recollections on what the win meant to us by saying, 'That set us up. That was two out of two and put us in a strong position. It was a big, big win and I think we needed a good start to galvanise everyone, and thankfully we got the two wins to put us in a healthy position to start with.'

Two home games, two wins and top of Group 2 – not bad for a team that was supposedly in crisis. With bigger challenges on the horizon, it was vital that Scotland started to shake off the hangover from Italia '90 by claiming maximum points from two of our main challengers for that solitary qualifying spot.

The road to Sweden had begun!

Familiar and unfamiliar territory

FOUR POINTS from the opening two home games was the perfect start to Scotland's bid to reach Euro '92. Now it was time to do some travelling.

The first away trip for the Tartan Army to enjoy was a return to familiar territory in Bulgaria, whom Scotland had faced in the previous European Championship qualifying, for the 1988 finals. The meetings between the two in that campaign were tight affairs; a forgettable goalless draw at Hampden being followed up by a 1-0 win for Scotland in Sofia courtesy of a Gary MacKay goal. It was one of the rare highlights for the Scots in that campaign, but it had devastating consequences for the Bulgarians as they lost out on qualification to the Republic of Ireland, despite the fact that they only required a point beforehand to reach the finals in West Germany. MacKay never had to buy a pint in Dublin ever again!

Long before the days of regular cheap flights, travelling to the south-east of Europe wasn't easy, and it was a very small number of Tartan Army followers who made the trip to Sofia as opposed to the potential thousands who'd make that journey in the modern era. Ronnie McDevitt confirmed this by saying, 'Bulgaria was not the most accessible of countries at the time, with only a couple of direct flights a week, plus it had been World Cup year, so there were only around 50 Scotland fans at the match.'

Although they subsequently failed to reach Italia '90 and were the pot three side in the group, this was a top Bulgarian team ready to embark on their golden era, and they showed their potential with a very impressive 3-0 win in Romania the previous month. Amongst their talented squad, they boasted a genuine world-class player in Hristo Stoichkov, who was establishing himself as one of Barcelona's top stars at that time. Stoichkov would go on to win the Ballon d'Or in 1994 after his role in helping Barça to four consecutive La Liga titles, a first-ever European Cup win followed by another final appearance and, arguably more famously, spearheading his country's historic run to the World Cup semi-finals, having been joint top scorer at USA '94 with six goals. Scotland were going to have to pay special attention to him if they were to pick up anything in Sofia.

Once again, injuries had forced Roxburgh to make several changes to his starting XI, with five alterations being required from the Switzerland game. Maurice Malpas returned at left-back ahead of Steve Nicol and indeed captained the side as Alex McLeish made way for Liverpool's Gary Gillespie. Malpas became the third different player to captain his country in as many games in the campaign. At the top end, Gordon Durie made his first start by replacing John Robertson, whilst Brian McClair displaced Murdo MacLeod in midfield. Like Brian Irvine and Robert Connor previously, MacLeod would not feature again in the Euro '92 campaign, despite being named in the squad for the next four qualifying matches, with his last international cap coming in a friendly match against the Soviet Union in March 1991. Other notable absentees from the squad were Paul McStay and Richard Gough; the latter still hadn't made an appearance due to persistent injury problems that had blighted him since the ill-fated match against Costa Rica at Italia '90, whilst McStay again was forced to withdraw through injury.

The final alteration also came in midfield where the injured Stuart McCall made way for Jim McInally. The Dundee United midfielder was earning his fourth cap for his country, and his first for over two and a half years. McInally would be entrusted with the task of nullifying Stoichkov, but it was one that didn't faze him given his experience at club level, having played an integral part in United's run to the UEFA Cup Final in 1987.

Reflecting on his international return, McInally said, 'That was my first cap for a wee while, that Bulgaria game. I think there had been a few injuries and a few call-offs and we had went out there a wee bit short of bodies, so that was me getting back into the squad and it kept me in it for a wee while up until the Euros. They were, obviously, a really good side, and my job in that game was to play against Stoichkov. I was always the guy that got the marking job, and you know what a fantastic football player he was. I just remember that game playing against him, it was just such a big game, the atmosphere in these countries was fantastic with the hostility and stuff like that; it was always good. I had good experience playing away in Europe with Dundee United, so I used to thrive on these types of environments. It was enjoyable, and that game in particular, because I was playing against Stoichkov, it was something that will always stick in my mind.'

Scotland team: Goram, McKimmie, Malpas, McInally, McPherson, Gillespie, Durie (Nevin 67), McAllister, McCoist, McClair, Boyd

With McInally concentrating on nullifying the threat of Stoichkov, the rest of the team got on with taking the game to the hosts, and they got off to the perfect start. Tom Boyd used his pace to good effect down the left-hand side and sent his cross deep to the back post. Goalkeeper Boris Mihaylov misjudged it, the ball bounced off a surprised Gordon Durie and broke kindly for Ally McCoist to tap home his second goal of the campaign.

Shaken up at falling behind, the Bulgarians responded by going on the attack and two quick-fire chances almost saw them draw level within six minutes. Firstly, Lyuboslav Penev worked his way into the penalty and clipped the ball over Andy Goram but watched in agony as it cannoned off the bar. A minute later, a Krasimir Balakov corner found an unmarked Nasko Sirakov six yards from goal. Fortunately for the Scots, his header went just wide of Goram's left-hand post.

Scotland could have doubled their lead on the half-hour mark, when a long free kick from Malpas was nodded down by Durie to McCoist. The striker overhooked his shot, but Brian McClair reacted to throw himself towards the ball in an attempt to head it into the net. However, his timing was just out and the ball flew over him and harmlessly wide for a goal kick. At half-time, the Scots were ahead and coping reasonably well in the hostile atmosphere inside the national stadium in Sofia.

The pressure cranked up in the second half as Bulgaria brought on Nikolay Todorov on 54 minutes to add an extra attacking dimension. His impact was almost immediate as he played a pass into Penev, whose touch took him beyond Gillespie before placing the ball past Goram. Fortunately, the linesman flagged for offside against Balakov behind him, although it is very debatable as to whether or not he was interfering with play. Either way, it was a huge let-off for the visitors.

Bulgaria now had Scotland on the ropes, with Todorov beginning to make an impact after his entry to the pitch. He then tested Goram a few minutes later with a powerful shot from the edge of the area, but the man known as 'the Goalie' to his team-mates was equal to it and parried it away from danger. Penev then had another opportunity as a long ball caught the Scottish defence off guard and he sneaked in behind on the left-hand channel, but his left-foot shot went just wide of the post.

Despite the pressure, the Scotland defence were coping reasonably well in the hostile environment and kept the hosts largely at arm's length. Then, with under 20 minutes to play, the Bulgarians got a break when Todorov's shot from the edge of the area deflected off a lunging Stewart McKimmie, over Andy Goram and into the net. Although there was disappointment that the Scots didn't hold out for victory, a draw was still viewed as a positive result, and five points from a possible six against the three main rivals in the group was a good return from those first three games.

By and large, McInally did an effective job on Stoichkov, to nullify his threats, though he does recall a scare in the first half caused by a short ball to him by Gillespie. Luckily, the Barcelona star blazed his shot over the bar to the relief of the midfielder. Expecting a grilling at half-time from Roxburgh, McInally was relieved to see that it was Gillespie who bore the brunt of Roxburgh's wrath. Ironically, despite being selected in the next three qualifying squads, Gillespie would not play for his country again.

McInally said, 'A funny thing that always sticks in my mind is, if you're talking about modern-day football, if you watch the way football is played now, being played out from the back et cetera, it's something I've always been a fan of – if you're good enough to do it then do it. But if you're not that type of player then don't do it. Andy Roxburgh was a lovely man, and he was good to me over the years with Scotland teams. Jim McLean had told me often enough at Dundee United that when we get the ball at the back to keep out of the road and let the good players get on the ball.

I always remember Gary Gillespie getting the ball off the goalkeeper and rolling a pass to me with my back to goal when I wasn't particularly looking, and before you knew it Stoichkov had robbed me and fired a shot over the bar. At half-time, rather than Andy Roxburgh get on to me, he said to Gary Gillespie, in the nicest possible way, "With all due respect, that's not John Barnes you're passing the ball to!" So that's something I often tell people, especially the way modern football is, because nowadays people like me, who weren't particularly good with their back to goal, still try and play and still do things that they aren't good enough to do, and I well knew my limitations by then off Jim McLean anyway, and I didn't need Andy Roxburgh to say to Gary Gillespie. I really enjoyed that game and it certainly got me back into the squad for the Euros.'

Scotland led the table with five points, one ahead of Switzerland, who had comfortably beaten debutants San Marino 4-0 away from home, with the Bulgarians one point further back on three. Romania had no points at this stage but got off the mark a month later with a resounding 6-0 home win over San Marino. The battle to top Group 2 began to heat up as 1990 drew to a close.

Before the next round of qualifying matches, Scotland were involved in a friendly at Ibrox against the

Soviet Union in early February 1991. Unsurprisingly, Roxburgh rung the changes for this one with seven in all, though this was no experimental line-up as several experienced campaigners returned to the fold. Richard Gough and Alex McLeish returned to central defence in place of McPherson and Gillespie. It was Gough's 51st appearance for his country and he was given the captaincy at the home of his club side, though it is not known that this gesture was in recognition of the fact that he didn't get to captain his country on his 50th cap against Costa Rica at the World Cup. It was common tradition for players to wear the armband on their 50th appearance for their country, but perhaps the World Cup finals was the exception to that rule as Roy Aitken led his team out in Italy. Steve Nicol came in at left-back, with Malpas switching to the right and the injured Stewart McKimmie dropping out. In midfield, Stuart McCall and Paul McStay replaced McInally and McAllister, whilst Robert Fleck came in for a rare start in attack in place of Brian McClair. This would be the last of Fleck's four Scotland caps and his only involvement in the Euro '92 story, whilst substitute Murdo MacLeod's international career also came to a halt after winning his 20th cap.

The final change saw the return of veteran Gordon Strachan in place of Gordon Durie. Having not played for his country since a 3-0 defeat to France in October 1989, Strachan made a shock return to the international set-up following an impressive run of form at Leeds United, who had won promotion back into the old First Division (nowadays known as the Premier League, of course) ten months earlier. Age was proving no barrier for the 34-year-old as he was excelling as Leeds skipper in their first season back in the top flight of English football, with his performances earning him the honour of the Football Writers' Player of the Year, thus becoming, to date, the only player to win the accolade both sides of the border. Strachan's form was too good for Roxburgh to ignore and he had no hesitation in bringing him back into the fold.

Scotland team: Goram, Malpas, Nicol, McCall (McAllister 69), Gough, McLeish (MacLeod 46), Strachan, Fleck (Durie 75), McCoist, McStay, Boyd (McPherson 46)

Like most friendlies, there wasn't much to write home about and the Soviets were closest to scoring in the first half when Igor Shalimov was put through by Sergei Yuran, only to prod his effort wide of Goram's left-hand post. Scotland rarely threatened, with the best effort being a long-range shot by McStay after a fine run, but his strike went wide of the right-hand post. Just as the game was petering out to an uneventful goalless draw, the Soviets stole victory when Andrei Kanchelskis laid the ball off to Dmitri Kuznetsov, who placed his shot neatly into the bottom-right corner of the net. Little did we know then that we would be facing these same players some 15 months later, although this would be the last match between Scotland and the Soviet Union as they would dissolve by the time 1991 came to a close. They would enter 1992 under a new guise, but more on that to come later.

Over a month later, Scotland welcomed the Bulgarians to Hampden for the return fixture of the November encounter. Four changes were made to the side that lost the recent friendly against the Soviet Union. Dave McPherson returned to the starting line-up in place of Steve Nicol, although he would have to be content with playing at right-back as Gough and McLeish were restored at centre-back, with Malpas switching to left-back. McLeish resumed the captaincy after Gough was given the armband for the previous game. Jim McInally also came back into the starting line-up in place of McCall, whose injury-prone season interrupted him again, whilst Gordon Durie came in on the left side of midfield for Tom Boyd. Brian McClair was restored in attack in place of Fleck.

Scotland team: Goram, McPherson, Malpas, McInally, Gough, McLeish, Strachan (Collins 80), McClair, McCoist, McStay, Durie (Robertson 80)

The return of Gordon Strachan had been noticed by the Bulgarians and Roxburgh knew that they would have special treatment in store to nullify his threat. BBC Scotland commentator Jock Brown, who is also the brother of Roxburgh's assistant Craig Brown, recalled that the Bulgarian's chief enforcer at the time was Ilian Kiriakov, who specialised in man-marking some of the best players in Europe (although, Aberdeen fans will tell you, this was not evident during his ill-fated spell at Pittodrie in the latter half of the decade). Although Strachan endured a frustrating evening, Jock revealed why the management team were satisfied with the role he played in order to allow others to flourish.

He said, 'Bulgaria identified Strachan as the man that they had to put under control, and Strachan was marked by this guy for the entire first half. He was told that would happen. Andy and Craig knew, having watched him inside out, and said to Strachan, "This guy will man-mark you." And Strachan said at the time, "I'm used to that all the time at Leeds; it's not a problem." But they said, "No, this guy's good at it, so you'll need to be dragging him about the park, looking for space and all that." They then went on with the first half. Strachan didn't get a kick. The guy tracking him never tackled him at any time; he stood all over him, prevented him getting the ball and intercepted every time they tried to give him the ball. Strachan came in at half-time utterly dejected, couldn't believe it and was sitting in the dressing room at half-time, not having had a kick at the ball, and saying, "I can't get into this game." Andy and Craig said, "We told you, that's all the guy does. You'll need to take him into places he doesn't want to go; you'll need to drag him all over the park, take him to the corner flags. Just take him out of the equation so the other guys can do things. This is a big compliment to you here." Strachan never got a kick the whole night and, at that time, he was our top man, and this was this one guy who man-marked him, and the guy never kicked him.'

Sporting their new navy-blue kit with a fancy white pattern on the right sleeve, white shorts and navy-blue socks, Scotland set about the task of getting the two points that would keep them in pole position at the midway point of the campaign. It was a tense affair as both sides cancelled out each other for the majority of the game, with both teams having one real clear-cut chance each in the first half. Firstly, the visitors carved an opening when Ivaylo Yordanov played a one-two with Nasko Sirakov, but he lashed his shot over the bar when one-on-one with Andy Goram. Towards the end of the half, Scotland so nearly opened the scoring when Durie's long throw bounced towards McClair, whose header was tipped on to the bar by Boris Mihaylov.

The second half was a similar tale, though Scotland were doing most of the attacking but being restricted to half-chances at best by a determined Bulgarian defence. With ten minutes to go, Roxburgh decided to make a double change, with Strachan and Durie making way for John Collins and the returning John Robertson. The gamble paid off within three minutes as Collins got in front of his marker to bullet home a diving header from McClair's cross to break the deadlock. It looked as though it was going to give Scotland a third consecutive home win over yet another of their main rivals for qualification, but then controversy struck in the final minute as Bulgarian substitute Lachezar Tanev appeared to be offside but was allowed to run through on goal. He was brought down by Goram, but the ball broke to Emil Kostadinov, who slotted home the equaliser, giving a repeat result of the previous meeting four months earlier.

Perhaps it was things evening themselves out from the disallowed Penev goal in Sofia, but nonetheless losing that goal was a real body blow that could've had huge consequences in the final standings, as two points were suddenly reduced to one. The nature of Kostadinov's equaliser was summed up by midfielder Jim McInally, who said, 'I'm pretty sure it was offside, and in modern day it would be given as offside. Bulgaria were a very good side. These games are always pretty tight and at that particular time, Bulgaria would probably be rated higher than us as a nation. I remember we missed a couple of good chances, and then it was a wee bit of a sucker-punch at the end, because if we'd held on to win that game, it would've certainly put us in a much more comfortable position than what we ended up in. I actually watched highlights of the game in lockdown [during the coronavirus pandemic], and it was actually quite a bit offside, the goal, when I'd seen it again.'

Andy Roxburgh was also disappointed to see that an extra point had disappeared in controversial circumstances and summarised by saying, 'You wonder what VAR [video assistant referee] would've done to that. Maybe if we'd had VAR we'd have won the match that night! I can always remember it because I was almost switching my mind to think about, "What do we say here at the press conference?" And the next thing, Kostadinov suddenly breaks away. That was a real sucker-punch, to lose that one in the last minute like that.'

Romania moved to within two points of the Scots with an expected, but hard-ought, 3-1 victory in San Marino that same evening. It was their next away trip the following week to Switzerland that was of more concern and it turned out to be a good night for the Scots as both teams cancelled each other out in a frustrating night at the Stade de la Maladiere, Neuchatel. The result kept Scotland top of the group on six points, a point clear of the Romanians and Swiss, with Bulgaria on four and San Marino pointless at the foot of the section. With three consecutive away trips to come, sitting top of the group at the halfway mark was a good position for the Scots to be in.

First up on the road was a trip to unfamiliar territory. San Marino, a small country based in northern Italy with a population of 24,160 at the time, were making their tournament debut since getting FIFA and UEFA affiliation in 1988, and several members of the Tartan Army took advantage of the opportunity to make their first visit to the nation.

For friends Roy Brunton, John Morrison and Steven Gardner, who are now part of the Beerhunters Tartan Army, the trip would be the first of many they would take together to follow Scotland across the globe. Back in the days before cheap flights via Easyjet and Ryanair, it wasn't easy to follow the men's national team abroad, and the methods to get to an unknown territory like San Marino were pretty complex. John said, 'For some reason, we stayed in the former Yugoslavia, which was Slovenia, and we hired two cars to drive from Slovenia to San Marino. I'm not sure of the mental state of us to do that! It wasn't an easy drive through places like Venice and Trieste; we had to do a U-turn on the motorway and things like that, and we got to Rimini, which was the nearest town to San Marino, then off to the match. That was the first qualifying match we went to together.'

Most of the Scotland fans who travelled were looking forward to some Mediterranean sunshine, which on 1 May 1991 wasn't an unrealistic expectation, so to then be welcomed with the kind of torrential rain they were used to back home would've been a shock, to say the least. The conditions caught out fellow foot soldier Ronnie McDevitt and his friends as they were caught up in a couple of unfortunate incidents, not that the weather dampened their enjoyment of the occasion.

Recalling the trip, Ronnie said, 'For the trip to San Marino, we had already decided to return to Genoa, where we had been based at Italia '90, and a few other Scotland fans had the same idea. The thing I remember most about San Marino was the torrential rain, which made the pitch difficult to play on, and it took a penalty kick in the second half to finally open the scoring. It had been quite decent weather earlier in the day and a lot of fans were wearing shorts, but the monsoon arrived an hour or so ahead of kick-off. I recall losing my footing and tumbling down a steep hill on the approach to the stadium and my clothes being covered in mud. Inside the ground we stood on what appeared to be a temporary wooden, slippery structure which I am sure would not pass the required safety checks today. It had no cover and ran along the length of the pitch, supporting around 2,500 of us. A friend of mine dropped his glasses and they fell through the gap in the wooden planks and he ended up with someone else's at the end of the game after searching around underneath the stand in the dark.'

Facing San Marino wasn't the only first for the Scotland men's national team that evening. It was also the first, and only, time that the white away kit with purple and red splashes across the chest was worn by the team, kicking off an age of debatable designs by Umbro. Stuart McCall wasn't a fan of the design, as he recalled, 'It didn't go with ginger hair, that's for sure! I've kept one of them in the loft, but it wasn't one of my favourite kits.'

As for the game, it was the usual multiple changes for Roxburgh from the last game – five of them in this case. Gough and McLeish missed out, and it turned out that the Bulgaria match would be the last we saw of Alex McLeish in a Scotland jersey for two years. A series of injuries would plague the veteran centre-half and this meant that his Euro '92 adventure was over. They were replaced in defence by the returning Stewart McKimmie and Steve Nicol, with McPherson and Malpas moving from full-back to be the centre-back pairing. McInally was ruled out through illness, so McCall came back into midfield, alongside Gary McAllister, who took the place of McStay, and skipper for the night Gordon Strachan.

For McInally, it was a big disappointment to be missing out on the trip to an unfamiliar part of the world, even if he knew he'd have been unlikely to start. He said, 'I pulled out of that squad with illness and I can remember that vividly because I was gutted because I was dying to go to that part of the world. I'd heard so much about it, how affluent it was and stuff like that. Not that I would've played anyway, because, throughout these games against the smaller nations when we needed to score a goal, I certainly wasn't going to play in games like that. I was in most of the squads, but I always remember that was one I had to pull out of because I was ill and I remember it because I was keen to see that part of Italy.'

Expecting to be on the front foot for the vast majority of the evening, Roxburgh went with a three-man forward line, with McClair and Durie being joined in attack by Kevin Gallacher, who was making his first Scotland appearance for two and a half years. Having been left disappointed at being omitted by Roxburgh for the World Cup squad nearly a year earlier, Gallacher was determined to do enough to ensure he wouldn't be left out again.

Scotland team: Goram, McKimmie, Nicol (Robertson 73), McCall, McPherson, Malpas, Gallacher, Strachan, McClair (Nevin 57), McAllister, Durie

The expectation of this being an easy night for the visitors proved to be false as the Scots struggled to get past a dogged San Marino defence and went into the half-time break frustrated that the deadlock was not broken. The sluggish performance continued early into the second half and it was looking like unexpected dropped points were going to happen.

Enter Pat Nevin!

The Everton winger came on for his long-term friend Brian McClair. His pace and trickery made an immediate impact. On 62 minutes, he won a penalty as he was brought down when in on goal. Strachan expertly converted by sending the goalkeeper the wrong way. Not lacking in confidence and with the knowledge that his manager knew he was capable of making the impact we desperately needed, Nevin recalled in his autobiography, *The Accidental Footballer*, 'I knew I could fix it. Andy Roxburgh often used me as the key to unpick those kind of intricate locks. There were always at least nine defenders between us and the goal, even when they were allegedly attacking, so it needed imagination. I came on, managed to wriggle through their defence and, as I was about to score, I was tackled agriculturally to win a penalty.'

Three minutes later, the crucial second goal arrived to put the game beyond doubt as Durie got on the end of a Strachan corner to head home. It was a struggle, but it was job done as Scotland got the two points to keep themselves a point clear of the Swiss, who came back from two down to win 3-2 in Bulgaria that same night.

Could you imagine the headlines had the unthinkable happened and Scotland not managed victory against a nation with less than 25,000 people in it?

Hugh MacDonald was working late as a sub-editor at the *Glasgow Herald* (now simply called *The Herald*) and his colleagues would've been preparing for those unthinkable headlines until the intervention of Nevin helped change the game. Although he didn't see the game, he was fully aware of what was going on. He said, 'I think that was the occasion of the great Ian

Archer in the press box in San Marino, which was high up on a mountain side, saying, "We're drawing nothing-each at half-time with a mountain top!" I was working that night as a chief sub-editor with *The Herald* at the time, but I can remember increasing anxiety looking at the watch. In those days there was no Twitter or minute-by-minute updates. I was updating Press Association Scorewire, or waiting for a shout from the sports desk saying that we'd scored – very dodgy moments out there. But the thing we come away with is a victory and you come away quite happy with the points in the bag.'

Despite the result, the press did give criticism to the players for the nature of the performance against the minnows. Steve Nicol was one individual who was singled out and it was allegedly supported by Roxburgh, which led to the 26-capped defender calling it a day at international level, although he would come out of this hiatus for one more game in the campaign, due to an injury crisis, to earn the last of his 27 caps. More on that to come in the next chapter.

In an extract from his autobiography, *5 League Titles and a Packet of Crisps*, which was serialised in the *Daily Record* in 2016, Nicol said, 'We scrambled a 2-0 win from a poor performance. I received some criticism from the press, which was fair. What I didn't expect was for Andy to publicly agree with them.

At Liverpool you were never criticised in public. In private? Absolutely. But for Andy to tell the press I wasn't at my best was unacceptable. He hung me out to dry. I think he chose this course of action because he wasn't experienced enough. Stein, Bob Paisley, Ferguson or Kenny Dalglish would never have done that – even if they'd gone right through me in private. Now, I'm the most mild-mannered person you could meet, but when someone says something about me that's not true, I become a totally different animal. I wasn't having that. "Don't you dare suggest I said anything about you," I replied. "In fact, just don't bother picking me for Scotland again.'" Switzerland then went top of the group by demolishing San Marino 7-0 in St. Gallen, with Bulgaria also defeating the minnows 3-0 away from home in between. Just over a year before the finals were due to kick off, the Group 2 table looked like this:

Pos	Team	Played	Won	Drawn	Lost	Points	Goal dif
1st	Switzerland	6	4	1	1	9	+13
2nd	Scotland	5	3	2	0	8	+4
3rd	Bulgaria	6	2	2	2	6	+3
4th	Romania	5	2	1	2	5	+4
5th	San Marino	6	0	0	6	0	-24

The four-point gap between the four main rivals emphasised how tight the group was, and three of the teams had a case of saying that fate was in their own hands if they won all of their remaining matches. Bulgaria were exceptions to that rule as even winning their final two matches against San Marino and Romania would not be enough to see them qualify, mainly due to the fact Switzerland, Romania and Scotland all had each other to play.

It really was between Switzerland, Romania and ourselves now, and we now had to play both of them away from home. The biggest challenge of our European Championship qualifying campaign was just around the corner.

Swissed off

SCOTLAND'S EURO '92 campaign had been simmering along nicely, but the pressure was now being intensified in Group 2 going into the final three matches.

A year on from opening the campaign with home games against Romania and Switzerland, it was roles reversed as we faced two crucial games within a month that, potentially, could have an impact on the men's national team reaching their first-ever European Championship finals.

First up was a trip to the Wankdorf Stadium, Bern, to face Group 2 leaders Switzerland. A point ahead, having played a game more, the hosts knew that victory could see them put one foot on the plane to Sweden, given the vastly superior goal difference they had over the Scots and the Romanians. For Andy Roxburgh, he knew this was a game Scotland simply couldn't afford to lose with the visit to Romania looming on the horizon.

Scotland were forced to make three changes from that victory in San Marino. Out went Gary McAllister, Kevin Gallacher and Brian McClair to be replaced by Tom Boyd, Ally McCoist and, most surprisingly, Mo Johnston. After Italia '90, it looked as though Johnston's Scotland career was over after he announced his international retirement at the age of just 27. However, he was persuaded to return to the fold initially for the Bulgaria match six months earlier, only to belatedly withdraw with injury. By bringing Johnston back in, Roxburgh hoped that he could rekindle the form that saw him score six goals in World Cup qualifying, which helped the Scots qualify for the finals in Italy a couple of years previously. Now back fit, and having started the season well at club level, Johnston was ready to lead the line again for his country alongside McCoist, who at the time was playing second fiddle to Johnston and English striker Mark Hateley at Rangers.

Another unexpected starter was Steve Nicol, who had told Roxburgh that he didn't want to be selected for his country again after their spat following the previous match in San Marino. However, a series of injuries in defence to the likes of Richard Gough, Alex McLeish, Gary Gillespie and Craig Levein led to Roxburgh reaching out for the Liverpool defender, who decided to temporarily come out of international-football hibernation to solve the problem. Nicol's inclusion forced regular right-back Stewart McKimmie into central defence to partner Dave McPherson, a role not too unfamiliar to him, having filled in that position for Aberdeen, caused by respective injuries to McLeish and Brian Irvine.

In an extract of his autobiography, *5 League Titles and a Packet of Crisps*, serialised in the *Daily Record* Nicol said, 'To say I was surprised when I received a phone call a few months later from Andy would be an understatement. He said, "We've had some call-offs and we need you for the trip to Switzerland. You're absolutely playing." I made it clear to him it was a one-off. I wasn't doing this for Roxburgh, I was doing it because I was asked to help out my country.'

Nicol's sudden recall might have raised a few eyebrows, but that was nothing to what the press reaction was like when news filtered through that Gough had to pull out with a thigh injury on the morning of the match. When the squad landed back in Glasgow after the game, the media were out in force to quiz him and Roxburgh about the withdrawal, and there were some accusations that Gough was giving a light-hearted approach to his country in comparison to his efforts at club level. In Gough's defence, he would also miss Rangers' next match against Dundee United three days later, supporting his assessment about the injury, although it's well-documented that he didn't feel supported by his national team manager at the time.

When I asked him about having to pull out of a team he was most likely going to be starting in, Gough simply said, 'I'd played on the Saturday and trained on the Tuesday and I didn't feel right to play. I said to Andy Roxburgh that I wasn't in a good enough condition to play and that was it. When we got back to Glasgow Airport, reporters were asking me why I'd pulled out on the day of the game or something. When you look back now, I think it was just reporters trying to get headline stories; that's what they wanted, you know.'

Scotland team: Goram, McKimmie (McClair 66), Malpas, Nicol, McPherson, Boyd, Strachan, McCall, McCoist, Johnston (McAllister 40), Durie

With a makeshift back line and a raucous home support firmly behind the Swiss, Scotland struggled to get to grips with the match as Switzerland dominated the early proceedings. The hosts thought they had taken the lead after just ten minutes, when Marc

Hottiger's cross was brilliantly finished by Stephane Chapuisat. Fortunately for the visitors, Nicol stepped up just in time and the linesman flagged correctly for offside. There was another scary moment on 23 minutes, when Alain Sutter let fly from 25 yards and had Andy Goram beaten all ends up. However, the crossbar came to Scotland's rescue and the ball bounced just the right side of the line before being cleared to safety.

Despite those two let-offs, Scotland did create two opportunities of their own either side of the Sutter effort, both falling to Ally McCoist. Firstly, he was picked out by a great ball over the top by skipper Gordon Strachan, but his touch let him down and was eventually crowded out by the Swiss defence. More glaringly, on 28 minutes, he was played through down the right-hand channel by Nicol and he beared down on Stefan Huber's goal. Instead of pulling the trigger, McCoist tried to go around the goalkeeper, who read his intentions and grabbed the ball from McCoist's feet. Perhaps a sharper and more confident McCoist would've taken advantage of those opportunities, but instead they were punished in brutal fashion as Switzerland raced into a two-goal lead.

Firstly, Hottiger's long pass caught the Scotland defence flat-footed, and Chapuisat sprung the offside trap to lash the ball past Goram to open the scoring. Everyone bar McKimmie stepped up, and McKimmie's lapse in concentration was duly punished in devastating fashion. Eight minutes later, the Swiss doubled their advantage when Chapuisat's corner was met by Heinz Hermann, who towered above McPherson to powerfully head home via the underside of the crossbar. It was a lead the Swiss deserved, having bossed most of the first half.

There was to be no fairy-tale return for Johnston as he lasted just 40 frustrating minutes before his night was ended after being accidentally knocked over by Gordon Durie, who was attempting to win a header from a Maurice Malpas cross. Innocuously, his knee caught Johnston in the back, resulting in an awkward landing for the Rangers striker. Johnston left the field with McAllister taking his place and, ironically, Durie moving alongside McCoist in attack.

A striker injured and two goals down at half-time, things were not looking good for Scotland. Meanwhile, the Swiss were looking good not only for the two points but for a place in the European Championship finals. Going into the half-time break, they believed the job was done.

Andy Roxburgh noticed this Swiss arrogance and used it as his half-time team talk to motivate his men into believing they could get something out of the game. He said, 'I got up off the bench to go in at half-time. We were two down. They're a very good team and played very well. It's not that we played badly, but they've got the two goals, they're the home team, there's 50-odd thousand there in Bern, and the thing is, as I got up to come and walk away, I just looked and I saw some of these players were celebrating. Now it's like a gut reaction – "It's half-time and they're celebrating!" And there's a long, dark tunnel that you walk up. It felt like a long, dark tunnel as we walk to the dressing room, and our players are sitting with their heads down. I just very quietly said to them, "Listen, lift your heads here. We'll win this match because they're celebrating, they think it's finished, they think it's over. If we score and it goes to 2-1, they'll become very nervous. All we've got to do is think of nothing else but score that next goal, because that will turn the tide here." So we changed a couple of things and absolutely went for it. We get that goal that turns the tide and our team just seemed to gain strength, and that 2-2 draw was the key element [to qualification].'

Roxburgh's words fired the players up. He made a tactical change by switching McKimmie to right-back and Nicol into central defence, and immediately the Scots got themselves back into the game after the restart. McKimmie went some way to atone for his error in Chapuisat's opener by sending over a delightful cross, and Durie's downward header nestled into the corner of the net. The half-time arrogance of the Swiss had now been knocked out of them and they became nervous, as Roxburgh predicted, which saw them drop deeper as the Scots took the game to them. Scotland even introduced another attacking option, bringing on Brian McClair for McKimmie, as they chased that crucial equaliser.

With seven minutes left, the Scots' perseverance was rewarded. Goram's long punt up the park was not dealt with by the Swiss defence. McCoist held off his marker to nod the ball down to Durie. His well-controlled half-volley was parried by the goalkeeper and it landed perfectly for McCoist, who drilled the ball under Stefan Huber to level the score and salvage a crucial point for Scotland. It was a huge relief for McCoist, given the two opportunities he had passed up earlier in the game at 0-0 that very nearly came back to haunt him, but that was forgotten about after netting, arguably, our most crucial goal of the campaign.

The effect of Roxburgh's half-time motivational speech was evidenced in that comeback, and we saw that this Scotland side had more ability, fight and determination than the first half showed. That draw would prove to be crucial in the overall standings. The players realised at the time that digging out a draw from the jaws of defeat against a side on the verge of qualification was significant.

Midfielder Stuart McCall summed up just what the result meant by saying, 'You always remember them games when you're 2-0 down, and I've watched that game back. I remember the dressing room after the game, because that was huge. And when you look at the league table at the end of it, if Switzerland had beaten us, we wouldn't have been at Euro '92. When you look back, the start was important, winning the two home games. The result against Switzerland was massive and I think that did show the camaraderie and the character within the group. To come back from 2-0 down at half-time, when it's looking lost, was huge. I'll be honest, I don't remember much about the game, but I remember afterwards the feeling and the euphoria within the dressing room. It's great when you come back from two down and you're wrote off, so that makes it special. When you get to the end of it, it was a huge, huge point.'

Fighting back from two goals down away from home to one of the main rivals for qualification emphasised the togetherness in this squad in a nutshell. Scotland could very easily have folded after half-time, but the team spirit that Roxburgh and Brown had created came through in that second period. The players proved that they would run through a brick wall for them by grinding out a crucial draw from what looked like an impossible position.

The character of the team is well summarised by Hugh MacDonald, who pointed out that the players were all playing to a high level with their respective club sides, which they brought to the national team, 'We had a lot of good characters in the team, a lot of good players but very good characters, and guys who were strong, not just with strong international experience but strong club experience. They played at a high level and played under real pressure of the then-Old Firm, pressure of English football, pressure of playing under Alex Ferguson at Aberdeen, and the pressure of playing under Jim McLean at Dundee United. This team wasn't a team of shrinking violets. You might've said they didn't have a stellar warrior of a Dalglish or a Souness, but it had very good players in it. Everything's subjective, of course, but I think in that team there were five or six very good players, maybe even including a couple of contenders for an all-time Scotland XI. A decent team who would come out in the second half with professional pride and go for it and achieved a smashing result.'

The Tartan Army who made the trip could be happy with their team's excellent comeback to salvage a point from an unlikely position, something that would've made the journey all the more pleasing. Jim Brown, chair of the Partick Thistle International Supporters Club – latterly changed to the more familiar West of Scotland Tartan Army (WESTA), having attracted fans of other clubs – summed up the relief by saying, 'I had organised a supporters' bus from Glasgow and 50 Scots on board were full of hope – well, until half-time. Two-nil down and we had not been playing well. But this is Scotland. Full time, 2-2, that bus bounced out of Switzerland and across France!'

Beerhunters Tartan Army boys Steven, John and Roy, who at this point travelled independently before joining the Beerhunters group, decided to follow up on their San Marino adventure by making the journey to Bern. Their half-time request to move from the home end to the away end proved to be a great move as they celebrated McCoist's equaliser, with Roy's celebrations being captured by photographers and his image used on the match-day programme when we returned to Switzerland for World Cup qualifying the following year.

Recalling the experience, Roy said, 'We walked into the Swiss end. There was two gates to go into: the home end and the away end. We actually had away-end tickets and slipped into the home end in amongst the Swiss. We were getting beat 2-0 at half-time and we asked the police, "Is it ok if we go into our own end, which is where we should've been in the first place?" They said "certainly", and opened the gates for us. We went in and it finished 2-2. It was absolutely brilliant. My photo was taken just after we equalised. I was on top of the fence, so when we played them after the Euros, the 3-1 game in Switzerland (World Cup qualifier for USA '94), on the front of the programme was a picture of me on that fence from the game before.' Recalling seeing his mate in that photograph, John simply pointed out to Roy, 'You looked like a hooligan!'

Switzerland may have remained top of the group by one point, but Scotland's fate was now very much in their own hands. If they could win their final two matches, away to Romania and at home to San Marino, they would be going to Sweden.

Next up was the trip to Bucharest to face Romania. This was a game the hosts simply had to win to stand a chance of overhauling the Scots and the Swiss; in fact, they had to win all three of their remaining games to reach the finals. A win was the preferred route for Scotland, though a draw would be acceptable if they could better Switzerland's result in Bucharest in the final round of matches.

Like the Bulgarian trip 11 months previously, it was a small contingent of Tartan Army followers who made the trip to another Eastern Bloc country, though this was up 200 from the Sofia trip. Ronnie McDevitt recalls how the country was adjusting after communist leader Nicolae Ceausescu was ousted from power two years earlier. He said, 'The Romania game coincided with a trade fair in Bucharest that same week and to secure accommodation we had to stay in a ski resort called Sinaia, which was not exactly a hive of activity in October. It was a bit of a ghost town really and I remember seeing cows casually strolling down the middle of the main street. The trip was nonetheless well organised, and we had a coach to take us to the capital and back, as well as airport transfers. This was just a couple of years after Ceausescu's fall from power and the country was still in transition. I guess I would have liked to have seen a bit more of Bucharest given the chance, as we have never played there since. In total there were 250 or so Scotland supporters in the country.'

Another fan who took in the trip was Grant Fisher, who had followed Scotland religiously, home and away, for nearly three decades before moving to Florida in 2006. He recalls Romania being up there with one of his most memorable trips, even if the local cuisine was a little peculiar.

Grant said, 'This was one of my most favourite trips ever. It was the first time I had really visited Eastern Europe. It was 1991, less than two years removed from the revolution and the overthrow of the Ceausescu regime. This was the first time I went with the official travel club – since visas and all sorts of paperwork were required to get into Romania, it was much easier to go with the official party. There were only a few hundred of us who went to the game, anyway. We landed in Bucharest and went by coach to a town called Brasov, up in the mountains of Transylvania. Beautiful town. I remember eating at a restaurant and we had meat – well, Gordon was a butcher and he sat there saying to me, "This isn't cow. It also isn't horse, which you get quite a lot in Europe." he said, "I don't know what this is." So he asked our server, who proceeded to raise his arms above his head and growl – we were eating bear!'

Having finished his bear meal, Grant then took in the European Under-21 Championship qualifier between the two sides, played at Stadionul Municipal in Pitesti, since renamed Stadionual Nicolae Dorbrin, after the 48-capped midfielder who played for local side Arges Pitesti. From 1976 until 2005, the qualifying campaigns for the under-21 version of the European Championship ran parallel with the seniors qualifying schedule for the Euros or World Cup, with the finals taking place biannually. Qualifying matches often took place the night before the seniors' game.

In this campaign, assistant manager Craig Brown took charge of the under-21s, in addition to his right-hand man role to Roxburgh with the main side. Brown's youngsters saw off their Romanian counterparts with an impressive 3-1 victory en route to qualification for their finals, where they reached the semi-finals. This under-21 side contained some exciting young players, many of whom went on to earn full international caps, such as Eoin Jess, Paul Lambert and Alan McLaren.

Recalling the experience of seeing Scotland under-21s in Romania and his thoughts on the talent the squad possessed under Brown, Grant said, 'I remember going to the under-21 match in the coach. Because we were with the SFA party, they waved us right into the stadium and we parked beside the official team buses. We never paid to get in. I assumed the SFA covered our entry, which I thought was generous, then I found out that tickets for the game were the equivalent of about 25p. That under-21 team was special; the best under-21 side I think we have ever produced. Three quarters of them ended up full caps – players like Lambert, Jess, O'Donnell, McKinnon, McLaren. It was a great side. I really thought they would win the Euros in '92. The quarter-final second leg versus Germany at Pittodrie is still the greatest match I have ever seen live – 3-1 down and win 4-3. Anyway, they beat Romania 3-1 and looked easy doing it.'

On to the day of the match, and the impact of the Ceausescu reign was there for all to see, with some buildings in the Romanian capital still showing damage from those dark times. Recalling that culture shock, Grant said, 'Then it was onto Bucharest for the big match. The capital was an eye-opener after tranquil Brasov. There were still bullet holes in the walls of a lot of official buildings. There was no electricity to power the city, so at night the streets were dark. It was quite unsafe and no way you should go out unless in large groups. The only places that were lit at night were the top bars and restaurants and the top hotels that had their own generators. I remember shopping in a local supermarket and being shocked by the change – the coins were so light, like they were made of aluminium; they felt like they would blow away if you tossed them up in a wind. And there were no small coins. If your change included small coins, they just gave you a sweetie instead. No 1ps or 2ps, but a penny chew will do. It was brilliant!'

It wasn't all about beer, football and sightseeing for the Tartan Army in Bucharest. Romania was in turmoil following the revolution, so much so that an estimated half a million children were in orphanages across the country. These orphanages were in poor condition and children often went cold, hungry and suffered horrible abuse from orphanage workers.

This prompted fans to make a donation of toys and gifts to a local orphanage, setting a precedent for future donations made by the Tartan Army Sunshine Appeal (TASA), which was formed in 2003 to make donations to children's charities across the globe. As of January 2022, TASA has made 87 consecutive donations from away trips the Tartan Army have made, bringing a smile to children's charities abroad. Recalling the 1991 act of generosity and what it meant for future donations, Grant Fisher said, 'I should say there was a collection from the fans for toys and gifts for the local orphanage. [I] almost feel it was the birth of the TA Sunshine Fund that is so important today.'

Whilst the Tartan Army were taking in Romanian culture and bringing smiles to the faces of Romanian orphans, Roxburgh was dealing with the frustratingly familiar injury crisis, with the defence being a particularly problematic area. For the second game in a row, Roxburgh had to persuade a player to temporarily come out of the international wilderness to help resolve the situation. Roy Aitken had stepped aside from international duty after leading his nation in Italia '90 but had told Roxburgh that he would return if deemed necessary. With Gough, McLeish and Gillespie ruled out and Steve Nicol going back into international retirement, Aitken answered his nation's call, albeit knowing that he would be a substitute for the game. He came on after 70 minutes to try to help the side earn a valuable point for what would be the last of his 57 caps before stepping aside again.

Speaking to the Official Scotland Podcast of the decision to temporarily end his international hiatus, Aitken recalled, 'I'd said to Andy after the World Cup in 1990, because I was with Newcastle at the time, "Look, I've done my time. You've got some great players coming through now. I'm not going to retire, but I'm here if you need me. But I'm going to take a step back to concentrate on club football. I was 31–32; not that old. I probably could've played a bit longer, but I just felt it was time for me to step back and take charge and plus spend more time with the family because, with the international team and European games, you're away virtually every week – trips here, three or four days there. So I said to him that I'll step back. I did my time with Newcastle, played there for a year and a half, came back up with St Mirren under Davie Hay in 91/92, and I think there was a shortage of players, and Andy called me in and says, "Look, would you come and sit on the bench for me and, if needed, I'll bring you on?" I said, "Sure, if you need that."'

With Aitken brought in as cover on the substitutes' bench, three changes were made to the side that drew in Switzerland, with a few tactical changes thrown in. Nicol's hibernation meant Stewart McKimmie moved back to his more familiar right-back slot, whilst Craig

Levein came in for his first international appearance since the 2-1 win over Sweden at Italia '90 to partner Dave McPherson in central defence. The front two also saw changes as injury deprived Roxburgh of the services of both Ally McCoist and Mo Johnston. Brian McClair was brought in to partner Gordon Durie, who was back in attack courtesy of his role in the Swiss comeback, having moved into his preferred position following the innocuous injury to Johnston. That left a gap on the right-hand side of midfield, which was filled by Celtic's Mike Galloway, who was making a surprise debut for his country due primarily to the withdrawal of McAllister.

Scotland team: Goram, McKimmie, Malpas, McCall, McPherson, Levein, Strachan, Galloway (Aitken 70), McClair, Durie, Boyd (Gallacher 59)

Scotland's aim was to keep a clean sheet and try to hit the Romanians when they could on the counter-attack to nick a goal that would put qualification in their own hands. Part one of the game plan was working for large spells as the hosts struggled to break down a stubborn Scotland rearguard, with just the one clear-cut chance created. Florin Raducioiu sent a cross to the far post that went over Maurice Malpas's head and was brought down well by Marius Lacatus. The winger evaded an attempted challenge by Stuart McCall, but then lifted his effort over Andy Goram and wide of the post. Despite that scare, Scotland were keeping the hosts at arm's length, but chances at the other end were few and far between and the sides went in goalless at half-time.

Romania then created the best chance of the game early in the second half. When skipper Gheorghe Hagi crossed from the right, the ball was flicked on by Lacatus perfectly into the path of Raducioiu. Somehow, from around six yards, the striker's volley was well saved by the legs of Goram and the Scots breathed a sigh of relief. The visitors created their only chance of the game when McKimmie won possession in the right-back area and sent Gordon Durie down the right flank. He then sent over a back-post cross, where substitute Kevin Gallacher stretched to volley for goal and the ball went narrowly wide of Silviu Lung's left-hand post. It looked as though the game was going to peter out to a goalless draw, with Scotland frustrating a host side on the front foot but struggling to get into the Romanian half. Given the circumstances, with the injury issues at the start, coming away from a hostile environment with a draw would've been a positive result, knowing the Swiss still had to visit Bucharest a month later.

Unfortunately, referee Aron Schmidhuber spotted a handball by Durie on 72 minutes and awarded the hosts a penalty. Durie protested that he was fouled as the ball came into the area but, with his arm above his head as he jumped, it was difficult to argue with the official. Up stepped talisman Hagi, who, despite Goram diving the right way, placed his kick brilliantly into the bottom left-hand corner to give Romania the win they desperately needed, and probably deserved, to keep their qualification hopes alive. For Aitken, it wasn't the temporary international return he had hoped for as he couldn't help his side hold out for what could've been a vital point. He said, 'I remember going to that Romania game and we lost 1-0. It was a tight game. It was a disappointing result. I came on in the last 25 minutes or something. So that was that. I stepped back again and I never went back in since then.'

It was the worst possible time for Scotland to lose their first match in the section. The players looked dejected, knowing that defeat meant that our qualification destiny was now out of our hands. McCall shared the frustrations of the players, saying, 'They had two or three outstanding players, so it was always going to be a difficult game. To go deep into the second half, 73rd-minute dubious penalty, it was hard to take. We knew after starting with two home games that we had two tough away games and we needed to take at least a couple of points. A point in Switzerland was great, but then to get beat by Romania was a blow and it almost took it out of our hands. It kick-started Romania. It took it out of our hands and it had gone from the elation of Switzerland to deflation. The mood of the country dipped a little bit because we were expected to go and get something.'

Assistant Craig Brown highlighted that the intimidating atmosphere in Bucharest made it a testing night, but that Scotland were coping well until the penalty incident, which he confessed to having no complaints over. In his autobiography, *The Game of My Life*, Brown said, 'The 30,000 home crowd played their part in cheering on their side, and we were grateful that we had done our defensive homework, because the Romanians worked hard to break us down and threatened to run riot if we caved in. We were doing fine, even though we were under intense pressure. Unfortunately, Gordon Durie lost his head momentarily in the 73rd minute and gave away a penalty when he handled in his own area. It was one of those things that can happen to anyone. Gheorghe Hagi, the Romanian superstar, scored from the spot and his side then shut up shop for the rest of the game. It was a blow to our qualifying hopes and we knew that we had to go for gold against San Marino in our final group game.'

On the same evening, Bulgaria eased to a 4-0 home win over San Marino in a dead-rubber affair. The night's events meant that the Group 2 table now read as follows:

Pos	Team	Played	Won	Drawn	Lost	Points	Goal dif
1st	Switzerland	7	4	2	1	10	+13
2nd	Scotland	7	3	3	1	9	+3
3rd	Bulgaria	7	2	2	2	8	+3
4th	Romania	6	3	1	2	7	+5
5th	San Marino	7	0	0	6	0	-28

Four teams separated by just three points shows how tight the group was, and that there was little between the teams in terms of quality. Although technically Bulgaria still could finish top of the group, they needed an unlikely sequence of events that included San Marino taking a minimum of one point from Scotland, Romania beating Switzerland, then defeating the Romanians themselves – all with a ten-goal swing to overhaul the Swiss to win the group.

Realistically, it was a three-way battle to see who would reach the finals in Sweden. Defeat in Bucharest meant that Scotland needed to win and hope that two other results went their way.

Qualification hung by the thinnest of threads.

History made in Sofia

THREE GAMES, two match days, one qualification place for the finals of the 1992 European Championship.

Scotland were still very much in contention for top spot in Group 2, but defeat in Bucharest the previous month took matters out of their own hands. Sitting a point behind Switzerland and two points clear of Romania, who had a game in hand, the Scots now needed to ensure there were no slip-ups in their final game against San Marino.

Not only that, they needed to win by a huge margin in order to overturn the ten-goal swing in the event of Switzerland drawing in Bucharest to overhaul them and qualify that evening. Realistically, the best scenario was Romania winning but then failing to beat Bulgaria away from home a week later to reach the finals. A Switzerland win would see them qualify and keep both the Scots and Romanians at home the following summer.

To put it simply, Scotland had to win and pray for good fortune in Bucharest and Sofia if they were to qualify.

Before a ball was kicked on 13 November 1991, there was a dispute over the kick-off time in both matches. Understandably, Romania and Switzerland wanted both games to kick off simultaneously, so that Scotland didn't have the advantage of knowing what they had to do by the time their game kicked off. However, the 2.30pm kick-off time that UEFA imposed was a big issue for the Scottish Football Association, given that the vast majority of their fans would be at work or at school, which would've severely impacted the attendance for such a vital game. In the end, common sense prevailed, as both games kicked off simultaneously at 7pm UK time.

The resolution to the kick-off time was music to the ears of the Scottish Football Association as a crowd of over 35,000 rolled up to Hampden Park that evening – a huge contrast to the paltry 12,000 that attended our campaign opener against Romania 14 months earlier. The Tartan Army arrived at the national stadium with the expectation of a convincing win against the weakest team in the group. Amongst those in the crowd that night was your author, who was attending his first-ever Scotland match, and I too was hoping to see a few goals. I was sat in the old south stand, almost in line with the 18-yard box, closest to the goal where the east stand was located, which would turn out to be a great view as Scotland attacked that end in the first half.

That expectation wasn't lost on Andy Roxburgh, who made five changes to the side that lost in Romania and picked a largely attack-minded team, in hope that they could dish out a thrashing on their opponents. Richard Gough came back in as captain in place of Stewart McKimmie to partner Craig Levein in defence, with Dave McPherson moving across to right-back. Gary McAllister and Paul McStay came in alongside Stuart McCall in midfield, with Gordon Strachan and Mike Galloway dropping out. Brian McClair and Tom Boyd also made way to allow John Robertson and Ally McCoist to form a front three with Gordon Durie. For Galloway, his part in the Euro '92 journey, and indeed his international career, was over after just one cap. It was also the last involvement in the campaign for Roy Aitken, after his cameo as substitute in Bucharest to aid an injury crisis, before going back into international hibernation to end his Scotland career after 57 caps. Little did Strachan know at this point that he too would play no further part in the Euros adventure, but more on that to come later.

Scotland team: Goram, McPherson (Johnston 46), Malpas, McAllister, Gough, Levein (Gallacher 59), McCall, Robertson, McCoist, McStay, Durie

Scotland went about their business from the off and went ahead after just ten minutes. McStay picked up the ball just inside the San Marino half and began running towards their defence. He played a neat one-two with McCoist, saw his shot saved by the goalkeeper, then reacted to send a looping header into the net.

That goal should've opened the floodgates, but the Scots found it difficult to break down the visitors' defence again as San Marino put everyone behind the ball. Just past the half hour, they found that second goal when McAllister's outswinging corner was met by Richard Gough. The skipper powered his header into the right-hand corner of the net to the relief of the home crowd. It turned out to be the last of Gough's six goals for his country and, whilst it doesn't hold the same recollections for the Tartan Army as more memorable ones against England and the 95th-minute winner in Cyprus, it meant just as much to the skipper as the previous five times he'd hit the back of the net for Scotland. He said, 'I played 61 times for Scotland, scored six goals, so my percentage was one in every ten, so it's always great. I always keep those goals in my memory. Two against Cyprus, one against England, one against Canada. Different levels of teams, but always memorable.'

Six minutes later, the game was ended as a contest. Malpas hooked the ball forward from the left down the channel for Durie, who took a touch before slotting home, despite the best efforts of a sliding San Marino defender to stop the ball crossing the line.

With the game effectively won, Roxburgh went after more goals in the second half in hope of clawing back the goal difference on the Swiss in the event of a draw in Romania. He even made the bold move of sacrificing two defenders, McPherson and Levein, for forwards Mo Johnston and Kevin Gallacher on 46 and 59 minutes respectively, which led to a 2-3-5 formation in the end. This turned out to be the last of Johnston's 38 appearances for his country as he'd now lost his place in the Rangers starting XI, ironically to McCoist. This led to him moving on to Everton for a less successful spell as his career started to go on a steady decline. Like the Switzerland trip two months earlier, it would be a frustrating half for Johnston, who was a pale imitation of the man of two years earlier who was firing Scotland to the World Cup in Italy.

Another man who was frustrated at Hampden that night was John Robertson. Desperate to add to his international tally as Scotland chased the goals, Robbo passed up multiple opportunities that could've helped close the goal-difference gap on the Swiss, should it come down to that. Recalling the game in his autobiography, *Robbo: My Autobiography*, the striker said, 'I was personally disappointed that I had passed up a golden opportunity to add to my Scotland total. I really should've walked away with the match ball as I had a couple of good chances saved. I headed one just past, blazed another over the bar and then had one knocked off the line by a defender. It was one of those games where I was simply not destined to score, whatever I did.'

Despite the attacking changes, only one more goal was scored, and it came on the hour mark. McStay picked the ball up 25 yards from goal and played a neat through-ball for McCoist, whose first-time shot went across the keeper and into the net for his fourth goal of the campaign. The 4-0 win may have been Roxburgh's biggest in charge of the Scotland men's national team, but it wouldn't be enough to overhaul the Swiss if they managed to get a point in Bucharest. Our hopes, as expected pre-match, now relied on Romania winning the game.

In the days before multiple live television matches, the internet and Sky Sports News, you would have to rely on the radio, Ceefax or Teletext to get up-to-date scores from other games, and updates from other international matches were even more difficult to get hold of at that time, particularly from eastern European nations. So for most of the Hampden crowd, they would have to wait until they got home to find out the result.

Fortunately, the scenario that we required to keep our hopes alive came true as Romania claimed a 1-0 win thanks to a Dorin Mateut goal, which eliminated Switzerland from the race for Euro '92. Everything now rode on the match in Sofia between Bulgaria and Romania a week later. The maths were simple – an away victory would take Romania to Euro '92 on goal difference; anything else and Scotland would reach their first-ever European Championship finals.

Bulgaria may have had nothing to play for other than pride and to start building for the World Cup qualifying campaign, but they would still be a tough nut for the Romanians to crack. Remember, they did comprehensively beat them in their own backyard 13 months previously. However, the Romanians now had momentum on their side, having gained maximum points from home games against the Scots and Swiss in the past month to catapult them into a position where they could claim their second European Championship finals appearance, having competed at Euro '84, which was held in France. They were confident of securing a third consecutive win that would see them complete the job and write another chapter of glorious failure for Scotland.

The game was of such significance that BBC Scotland made a last-minute decision to show highlights of the game on *Sportscene*. Commentator Jock Brown, who also worked as a lawyer, was asked on the morning of the game if he could do the commentary from their then-headquarters at Queen Margaret Drive in Glasgow's west end. After answering the call, Brown arrived to do his duties but encountered some obstacles to make life more difficult, including a long delay for the team line-ups to arrive! Luckily, previous knowledge of covering the two sides in their respective matches against the Scots came in handy to get him through the game.

Recalling that eventful late afternoon, Brown said, 'I got a phone call in the morning, I was at work at the time, saying, "Can you come in this afternoon? We've got the rights to Bulgaria v Romania and we're doing it off-tube." So I ended up doing it in a studio in Glasgow. It was a four o'clock kick-off our time, so I went in about three o'clock and I said, "How are we getting the teams sent to us?" We were told that one of the reporters at the *Glasgow Herald*, who was at the game, was going to phone the teams through in advance. The teams came through at five past five!

So the game's kicking off and I've no teams. I have no idea what the teams are. But remember, I've done the Romania v Scotland games and I've done the Bulgaria v Scotland games, so I'd done my homework for them and I'm now depending on recognising the Romanians and the Bulgarians. If I remember correctly, it was a soaking-wet night and the players who were blond at the start were not blond in ten minutes because the rain was coming down, and every time someone tackled there was mud on their shirt, so it covered their numbers. It was a nightmare! I had to take a chance at the ones that I could recognise, so Hagi and Stoichkov got a lot of kicks of the ball and I had to fudge it and busk it in the days of no co-commentator, on your own. Anyway, I got the teams at five past five, and I'm scrambling looking down at them and I realised that I hadn't named anybody who wasn't playing. In those days, it was routine to have these technical issues for important games, especially in the Eastern Bloc, when you're behind the iron curtain. You were in the lap of the gods.'

So the scene was set in Sofia, and the Tartan Army back home became Bulgaria fans for the night. Ironically, Scotland had beaten the Bulgarians four years previously, preventing them from qualifying for Euro '88 thanks to a Gary MacKay goal that sent the Republic of Ireland through at their expense. Would fate decree that they would lose (not intentionally, of course) and see us miss out on Euro '92?

It wasn't looking good in the first half as a confident Romania came flying out of the traps. They had an early goal by Adrian Popescu controversially disallowed for offside after he'd played a one-two with Marius Lacatus before slotting home. The replays showed that it was Florin Raducioiu, who wasn't involved in the play, who was offside and that Popescu actually beat a defender just before he scored. They were then handed a penalty kick on 18 minutes, when Bulgarian goalkeeper Boris Mihaylov brought down Raducioiu. Unbelievably, Gheorghe Hagi had his spot kick saved as Mihaylov atoned for giving away the penalty. It looked as though the footballing gods were conspiring against the visitors.

On the half-hour mark, their luck changed as Popescu sneaked in behind the Bulgarian defence again to prod the ball past Mihaylov, only this time the flag stayed down. At last, Romania had their goal and they were looking good for an away win and, more importantly, qualification to the Euros. For Scotland fans who were refreshing their Ceefax pages to keep up to date with the score, an agonising 45 minutes lay ahead as our Swedish dream was firmly in the balance.

Seven minutes into the second half came the moment that ensured that history would be made by the Scotland men's national team, with a little help from Bulgaria. Nasko Sirakov picked up a pass inside the penalty area and coolly placed the ball past Romanian keeper Silviu Lung to level the score. Try as they might, Romania couldn't find a late winner to turn the tide back in their favour. The game petered out to a 1-1 draw, which meant one thing …

SCOTLAND HAD QUALIFIED FOR THE EUROPEAN CHAMPIONSHIP FOR THE FIRST TIME IN THEIR HISTORY!

Great Scotland teams of the past, regulars at World Cup finals, with legends like Denis Law, Kenny Dalglish, Willie Henderson, Jinky Johnstone, Archie Gemmill, John Greig and Willie Miller, to name a few, had all tried and failed to take Scotland to a European Championship. Now the class of the Euro '92 qualifiers had become history-makers, and the Group 2 table clarifies this.

Pos	Team	Played	Won	Drawn	Lost	Points	Goal dif
1st	Scotland	8	4	3	1	11	+7
2nd	Switzerland	8	4	2	2	10	+12
3rd	Romania	8	4	2	2	10	+6
4th	Bulgaria	8	3	3	2	9	+7
5th	San Marino	8	0	0	8	0	-32

Without doubt, the happiest and most relieved man in Sofia was Andy Roxburgh. The Scotland manager had gone through a traumatic 90 minutes, praying for the outcome he had wanted, sitting in the stands with worry as the game – and qualification – hung by the thinnest of threads. Speaking in an interview we conducted for *Famous Tartan Army Magazine*, Roxburgh summarised the emotions he went through in the National Stadium, Sofia, and how grateful he was to a Bulgarian side whom we had given heartache to four years earlier.

He said, 'It was like an out-of-body experience in a way, because I sat in that stadium, with no control over what was going on, and literally had to watch it play out. It was as simple as that. I remember saying to some of the Bulgarian colleagues, "I really have to thank you," a bit like the Republic of Ireland had to thank us for getting them to the Euro in '88 because of what we did in Bulgaria as it turned out. In the first half, it was all one-way traffic, it was Romania, and they were the ones who were going to win that game that would've knocked us out. At half-time, whatever was said, Bulgaria came out in the second half and decided that their fans weren't getting what they should be getting, and so they upped their game and Scotland had qualified. It was the most nerve-wracking experience I've ever had, because I wasn't involved with either team, so it was a very strange night in Sofia, Bulgaria.'

Another nervous spectator back home was Stuart McCall, who was asked by a newspaper to watch the game in a studio so they could capture his reaction, whatever the outcome. The occasion mattered so much that he left an afternoon social event with his Rangers team-mates early to do the job, but now he could have a double celebration, with the knowledge that his country had qualified for the Euros. He said, 'I used to do a weekly newspaper column and they wanted me to go and watch the game in a studio, film me and get my reaction. Unfortunately, it was the same day as one of the Rangers players' birthdays, so we were going out for lunch, and you're not allowed to go out for lunch and have a couple of fresh oranges. So I had to have a couple of beers and I was a bit nervous watching the game, and we wanted anything but a Romania victory. Romania scored, and at half-time they're one-nil up. It was borderline, and thankfully Bulgaria equalised. It was everything – it was relief, it was jubilation, it was realisation. Often with Scotland, when you want things to happen, there's always something gone against us to get us through to next stages at major tournaments and things, but this was one result that went our way. It was fantastic. They took a picture of me with my tartan scarf on, watching the game, having a sly little beer – just like a fan, basically. I was watching the game live in the studio and it was a nervy, nervy experience, but one that turned out fantastic and I think I celebrated long into the hours!'

Whilst the players and manager were taking delight in qualification, the scale of the achievement was not fully recognised by the media. Yes, there were back-page headlines and stories recognising that Scotland had qualified, but the fact that this was our first-ever qualification for a European Championship was almost glossed over by an industry that was used to writing about the latest successful journey to reach a World Cup finals.

This was a point emphasised by Hugh MacDonald, who was chief sub-editor at the *Glasgow Herald* at the time. Qualification to our first European Championship was not viewed as a major achievement. It was an expectation from a nation who reached five consecutive World Cup finals, and it was long before the days of cover-to-cover dedication that followed Scotland's first qualification to any finals in 23 years when we defeated Serbia to reach the delayed Euro 2020. Hugh said, 'Everything's of its time. You would have something on the front page, and you would have it as the back-page lead etc. But you wouldn't have an outpouring of joy like with Serbia, with papers devoting page after page after page to it, for two reasons: one the media was traditionally restrained then – certainly in the broadsheet, football was not considered as important as it should've been. There was a very snobbish blind spot for papers like *The Herald* and *The Scotsman*, I felt. I was chief-sub at *The Herald*, I was part of the decision-making there at that time, and it was very difficult to force a football story's prominence, whereas nowadays it's back to front on football and football sells the papers now. The other thing of course was: a) it was the Euros, so it wasn't quite the World Cup, and b) it wasn't breaking a drought; we were pretty regular qualifiers. So, while there would be joy, it wasn't joy uncontained. It was, "This was great, we've done it, great, good," but not the sort of outpouring we would've had if it had been post-Serbia.'

Qualification for a first-ever Euros may have been glossed over by the media, but the scale of the achievement didn't go unnoticed by the fans. Ronnie McDevitt was one who recognised that qualifying for an eight-team European Championship was just as significant as being one of 14 European nations to qualify for World Cups in Spain, Mexico and Italy, particularly as Scotland lagged behind their rivals in previous qualification campaigns. He said, 'It was a big deal to reach Euro '92 as Scotland had never come remotely close to qualification before and had not even finished runners-up in any of the qualifying groups. For France 1984, for example, Scotland won their opening match then failed to secure another victory throughout the campaign and there was a feeling the SFA placed greater importance on reaching the World Cup, with the Euro qualifiers perhaps viewed as a practice run. Another theory offered was that the players only peaked every four years and if that coincided with World Cup qualification it seemed wise not to tamper with this cycle. You also have to factor in there were only a total of eight finalists in Sweden, which made it more of an achievement, so full credit to Andy Roxburgh for that campaign.'

As Ronnie highlights, Roxburgh deserves full credit for becoming the first manager in the history of the Scotland men's national team to not only qualify for a European Championship but for becoming the first to lead Scotland to two consecutive major international tournaments. It was just reward for a man who was appointed under a cloud of criticism from the media, with jibes of 'Andy who?' being circulated in the press.

What goes largely unnoticed is that Roxburgh led the under-18 side to their equivalent of the European Championship in 1982, beating Czechoslovakia in the final. He also took Scotland to the Youth World Cup a year later in Mexico, where they beat the hosts to advance to the knockout rounds in front of 86,000 people in the Azteca Stadium thanks to a goal by a certain Steve Clarke. Six members of that youth squad – Dave Bowman, Brian McClair, Jim McInally, Dave McPherson, Paul McStay and Pat Nevin (who scored in the '82 under-18's Euros final) – would go on to be included in the Euro '92 squad. That success did not go unnoticed by the SFA, and now they could feel justified by making that decision following qualification to consecutive tournaments.

On reflection, his appointment was a stroke of genius by the SFA for appointing a manager who was very successful with the underage teams. It is an opinion that is shared by Hugh MacDonald, who added, 'Roxburgh is a fascinating story. All the time, we regard the SFA as awkward, backward, stuck in their ways and not open to change. Looking back, Roxburgh was a terrific appointment and one that really made sense, but this was looking back. He was one of the first to attack diet and to try things like team customs, for example, in what was acceptable as a team and what wasn't. And, of course, being the front runner, he came across terrific resistance from parts of the press – "Andy who?" and all that. The press viewed it as a cop-out by the SFA by giving it in-house to this glorified Janny that would do their bidding, and it was quite the opposite. Can you imagine a book about Roxburgh now? He's advising the Asian Federation in his late 70s. He's led UEFA courses. He's had a terrific life, but at that time he was viewed, certainly by the press, as very dodgy, didn't know anything. The punters would not be used to having that in those days and you at least had to be a footballer. They knew you didn't have to be a great footballer. Andy, with his modest pedigree, was kind of looked down on amongst the fans. What worked for Andy was that the vital players in the team had come through as kids underneath him, so they had the respect of him. Generally, he had a decent reception from the players given his lack of pedigree, and his accomplishments were pretty significant.'

So that was the story of Scotland's journey to their first-ever European Championship finals. It was a journey that began in a wave of apathy on the back of yet another frustrating World Cup that ended in another early exit and ended in joy, following a fortuitous result in Sofia. Roxburgh had used no fewer than 28 players throughout the course of the campaign, which indicates how often he had to deal with injuries and the change in a player's circumstances, whether it be an international hiatus or a loss of form. Central defence became the biggest issue as there was a different partnership for each of the eight games, and there were five different players who captained the side at various points in the campaign – Paul McStay,

Alex McLeish, Maurice Malpas, Gordon Strachan and Richard Gough.

Of those 28 players, only Andy Goram played in all eight qualifiers, with Dave McPherson, Maurice Malpas and Gordon Durie next up on seven (Durie's includes one substitute appearance), and Stewart McKimmie, Ally McCoist and Gary McAllister on six (the latter also includes one substitute appearance). Only three other players played in more than half of the qualifying matches – Stuart McCall, Tom Boyd and Brian McClair (Boyd and McClair's stats include one substitute appearance each). Ironically, the two most-capped players in the squad that went to Euro '92, Richard Gough and Paul McStay, only played in five qualifiers between them (McStay three and Gough two), such was the injury issues both players had during the course of the campaign. They would make up for lost time during the finals with some impressive performances in Sweden.

Not many would've acknowledged at the time that we were up against three really tough opponents who were ready to go onto better things at the next World Cup in the USA two and a half years later. Switzerland came through a tough qualifying group that included Italy, Portugal and ourselves to qualify and then reach the last 16, Romania defeated Argentina en route to the quarter-finals, whilst Bulgaria eliminated France in qualifying and ousted defending champions Germany in the quarter-finals before finishing a credible fourth in the tournament.

For now, though, this was all about Scotland entering uncharted territory as we entered the draw for the 1992 European Championship finals. Things were about to get very tasty as we learned our fate for Sweden.

A champion draw

ON 17 January 1992, the draw for the ninth European Championship finals was conducted in Gothenburg. Representatives of hosts Sweden and the seven nations who qualified for the finals waited in anticipation to see who they would face that summer in their quest to be European champions.

There were two sides in the draw for the first time – host nation Sweden and, of course, Scotland. It was an exciting time for Andy Roxburgh after becoming the first manager in the history of the Scotland men's national team to qualify for the Euros. Now he attended the draw with members of the SFA hierarchy to see who we would be drawn against for the finals in June 1992.

Six other nations had reached the finals to complete the line-up, and each represented their own strong case to say they could win the tournament.

Holders the Netherlands, world champions Germany, semi-finalists from Italia '90 England, quarter-finalists at that same World Cup Yugoslavia and a resurgent France side who had won all eight of their qualifying matches.

Lastly, there was the Soviet Union, only now under a new guise called the Commonwealth of Independent States (CIS). This was because the Soviet Union had dissolved in December 1991 leading to the independence of several Soviet states. In football terms, ten new nations, including Russia, Ukraine, Belarus and Estonia, to name a few, would be competing in international competition going forward. This proved to be a big factor in the expansion of the European Championship from eight to 16 teams for the next finals in 1996, though at the time the bid process was based around an eight-team event. The landscape of Europe as we knew it at the time was changing.

For now, UEFA allowed the original Soviet Union side that qualified to enter as the CIS to complete the line-up for the Euro '92 draw.

The format for the draw was pretty simple. There were two groups of four, spearheaded by hosts Sweden in Group A and holders the Netherlands in Group B, whilst the other six sides went into an open draw and were not split into separate pots determined by world rankings that you see commonly these days with both the Euros and World Cup. With such strong sides in this field, the possibility of Scotland being drawn in a 'Group of Death' scenario was very high.

What we got was arguably the most daunting of groups imaginable!

Firstly, Scotland were drawn in Group B, which automatically meant that they would be paired with the defending champions, the Netherlands. The Dutch recovered from an abject showing at Italia '90 to come through their qualifying campaign ahead of a Portugal side who were starting to show signs of becoming a top European international team in the future. Above all, they still possessed the talents of AC Milan trio Ruud Gullit, Frank Rijkaard and Marco van Basten, who were key to their glory in West Germany four years earlier. They also had an emerging young star by the name of Dennis Bergkamp, another product of the famous Ajax youth academy, to add to the talents already at their disposal.

Next out of the hat came the CIS, formerly known as the Soviet Union. Like the Dutch, the Soviets also recovered from a poor World Cup performance to qualify for Euro '92, ahead of the Italians, who had finished third in their own World Cup. It should also be mentioned that the Soviets had reached the final in Euro '88, before going down 2-0 to the Dutch in Munich (ironically, after beating the same opponents in the opening game of the group stages) and still contained a few members of that squad, which included Rangers pair Oleg Kuznetsov and Alexei Mikhailitchenko. In addition, the Soviets had also beaten the Scots in a friendly at Ibrox in March 1991, so the challenge facing Scotland against a side under the new guise of the CIS was a tough one.

If coming up against the two finalists from the previous Euros wasn't hard enough, the last side out of the hat was reigning world champions Germany. Having won the World Cup less than two years earlier – as West Germany, shortly before the reunification with East Germany – the Germans contained many of the squad that powered their way to glory in Italy, including Jurgen Klinsmann, Andreas Brehme and Rudi Voller. They would be without their captain and talisman Lothar Matthaus, who missed the finals through injury, but the Germans still boasted a formidable squad who expected to add the European Championship trophy to sit alongside the World Cup. That said, they didn't have things all their own way in qualifying, going down 1-0 to Wales in Cardiff before beating them 4-1 at home on their way to reaching the finals. The Germans were managed by a certain Berti Vogts, who would be in charge of the Scotland men's national team a decade later but for now would be plotting the Scots' downfall as he sought to win a third European Championship for his country.

Of all the possible scenarios that Andy Roxburgh and Craig Brown could've played out, this undoubtedly was the toughest imaginable. Not that Group A was much easier, given it contained a strong Sweden side about to embark on a great journey of their own, a France side fresh from winning all of their qualifying games and amongst the favourites to win the tournament and an England side that, although missing the injured Paul Gascoigne, still possessed a squad capable of advancing into the latter stages of the tournament. It should also be mentioned that the other team drawn in this group at the time, Yugoslavia, were a very strong outfit that contained the talents of Darko Pancev and Robert Prosinecki, who were pivotal in the Red Star Belgrade side who became European Champions in 1991. Little did we know at this point that Yugoslavia would then be withdrawn from the tournament, but more on that to come.

Any three-team combinations of those four sides would've been a tough ask for Scotland to qualify from, but not as daunting as having the world champions, European champions and European runners-up in the one group! A lot of observers would've been worried by that challenge, but not Roxburgh and Brown, who relished the prospect of coming up against the biggest hitters in international football.

Reflecting on the draw, Roxburgh said, 'Our attitude was that, having got to the finals, we had nothing to lose. There's also this strange thing about Scottish teams, as our fans will know, we actually like to play against the big guns, because we always feel that we're better when we play against good teams. It gets everybody going. We have this strange mentality for a David-v-Goliath approach that we actually think when we're playing against big teams that we'll compete with them. Of course, there was the world champions, the current European champions, there was the Soviet Union, who'd won the Euros [in 1960] and were the previous finalists, so you couldn't have got a tougher draw. But our attitude was "let's see how this goes".'

Brown was equally bullish about the prospect of facing arguably the two best sides in Europe and taking on the likes of Gullit, Klinsmann and co. but acknowledged the size of task to qualify was enormous. In an interview we conducted for *Famous Tartan Army Magazine*, Brown said, 'We were saying bring it on and nothing to lose and, of course, it was a very demanding assignment. But it was to be enjoyed and we weren't in any way afraid of the opposition. That was never, in my time, an awe of opponents and certainly not, what I would say, mid-European countries.'

If Roxburgh and Brown were remaining calm, the Tartan Army were getting excited about the finals even more, with the mouth-watering prospect of facing such high-calibre opposition. This was a trip that was not to be missed, so those who could go got their travel plans in place.

What we have to remember was that there was no internet back in 1992, so there were no cheap flights online or discounted hotel sites that everyone could access. Travel agents were very much the way to go if you wanted to book a flight to Sweden, or wherever else the fans wanted to base themselves.

One such fan was John Wallace, who discovered an advert in one of the main newspapers for a package that he and a friend quickly took advantage of. He said, 'Me and my best mate had gone to the home qualifiers and joined the Travel Club, which was a tenner then.

'We saw an advert in the *Sunday Mail* for ten days in Sweden. The company was Bisland Travel and, from what I remember, cost was about £450 for flights and accommodation. It was booked over the phone; my mate paid the deposit and I gave the money to him. This was booked around February or March before the tournament.'

Fellow supporter Jim Brown was chair of the Partick Thistle International Supporters Club, now the West of Scotland Tartan Army (WESTA), at the time of qualification. Knowing that flights were limited, he and a few members discussed the idea of a coach trip to Sweden. In the days before Google Maps and sat nav, they had to work out the best route using an atlas and a paper road map of the Scandinavian nation.

Recalling the organisation of their trip, Brown said, 'At the time, airline travel was prohibitive. It usually required staying over a Saturday night to get any form of discount, so coach travel was the norm, no matter how far away it was. A group of us sat in the pub around a map of Europe and a road map of Sweden, along with hotel directories obtained from the local library. We identified the host cities and looked at possible alternatives for accommodation and travel. Then it was on to the fax machine, sending out messages to hotels, speaking with our bus companies and then phoning or mailing supporters with the thoughts. We very quickly filled our coach.'

Ally Wilson also took the bus route to Sweden, and revealed that ferry companies' reluctance in taking UK-based fans across to Scandinavia led to a lengthier journey as opposed to crossing the North Sea. He said, 'I saw an advertisement in a newspaper for a bus to

Sweden leaving from Glasgow. It would take 39 hours to get to Sweden, because the bus had to go via France, Belgium, Holland, Germany and Denmark. The ferry company sailing across the North Sea would not take footy fans. I think some Dutch fans wrecked a ferry while travelling to a European club game in the UK a few years before.'

If getting to Sweden was a complex matter, getting tickets for games was also a more straightforward process. As opposed to an era where the Scotland Supporters Club has more than 20,000 members, with a points system in place to determine who gets priority for away matches and first refusal for the delayed Euro 2020 finals matches, the scheme in place 30 years ago was the Scotland Travel Club. This had so few members that getting a ticket for the three games was much easier than the modern era, and the process to get the tickets was a lot smoother than tens of thousands crashing an online system the second tickets went on sale.

The Travel Club was administered by one person – Marjorie Nimmo. With so few people to contend with, compared to the team of people who deal with the Scotland Supporters Club, Marjorie would deal with ticket applications single-handedly and knew almost everything about each member before she even met them. Kevin Donnelly tells the story of his first encounter with Marjorie in Norrkoping and the personal touch she provided, whilst emphasising the difference between getting tickets in the 90s and the present day.

'They would send out forms,' he said. 'You've got to remember, it wasn't that big. If you look at that three-second game in Tallin, you'd be lucky if there were 350 fans there, 400 max. Now it could be two to three thousand. The first time I ever met Marjorie Nimmo, who ran the Travel Club, was in a tourist information office in Norrkoping when I was informed there were no hotels or bed and breakfasts or hostels in Norrkoping, and you'd have to go out to the wild to fend for yourself. So I met Marjory Nimmo. I'd never met her or spoken to her before. And she said, "Ah, yeah, are you Kevin Donnelly, travel member number 26, 5 Margaret Court, Winchmore Hill, London?" I turn to my mates and say, "How does this woman know everything about me apart from my inside leg measurement?" So many people at that time when they first met her, she'd just reel off the details, because she would be doing all the addressing the envelopes and stuff like that, and printing off labels to stick them on to the envelopes and sending the stuff out. She did it all herself for every game. In terms of personal service, a much smaller crowd of people actually going to the games. There were a lot of people who would go to tournaments but not go to qualifiers. You'll get your hardcore that go all the time, but other people will see we've qualified and then try to get a ticket, and I think tickets were relatively easy to get. I don't remember struggling to get a ticket.'

It wasn't just the fans who were getting excited by the prospect of facing three of Europe's best sides. The players too were relishing pitting their wits against some of the best players in the world.

Stuart McCall was all too aware of the size of the task ahead, and that there were preferred options from the seven available, but was not afraid to come up against tough opposition. He said, 'Whoever we were going to get, we were going to be underdogs. England were in there, we could've got the hosts Sweden, but it was a bit of both. It was, "Ooft, we're going to have to be at our best," but there was also a bit of excitement playing against the best players, and that's what you want to do really. So nearer the tournament it got more exciting, to be honest.'

Fellow midfielder Jim McInally was equally as excited when the draw came out, and not just from a player's point of view as he recognised the appeal of the hosts to the Tartan Army. He said, 'You had the best two teams in Europe, plus Russia could've been anything on their day – I would say a far better Russia team to what they are now. To be amongst all these guys and to qualify for that tournament, especially in such a nice country like Sweden, and a country that was accessible for Scottish supporters and stuff like that, it was just brilliant.'

The excitement in coming up against the world's best was there for all to see, but there was also a realistic view about Scotland's chances, that they would have to play above themselves to have any chance of upsetting the odds. Central defender Richard Gough, who would go on to captain the Scots in Sweden, was all too aware of the quality of the Dutch and Germans in particular, so much so he expected them to be battling it out in the final of the competition.

Analysing our prospects and who he thought beforehand would be the main contenders for the European Championship, Gough said, 'We were definitely going in as underdogs, put it that way! I just thought to myself, with the quality of players the Dutch had, you would've thought they would've got to the final. The two teams in our section, you thought they were favourites to go all the way. You could've said maybe France had a wee chance, or England even, but the two teams in our section I would imagine were the favourites because they had the best players.'

With the draw out of the way, the preparations for Scotland's inaugural European Championship finals appearance could now begin, and the SFA arranged two home friendly matches to take place in February and March 1992. First up was the visit of Northern Ireland on 19 February.

Roxburgh used the opportunity to give debuts to two players who were having impressive seasons at their respective clubs. Left-back David Robertson was rewarded for a fine first season at Rangers, following his move from Aberdeen, with his first cap in a back four with former team-mate Stewart McKimmie, his captain at club level Richard Gough, and future club team-mate Dave McPherson. At the other end, Hibs striker Keith Wright was given a start alongside Ally McCoist after impressing in his first season with his boyhood team, including a League Cup Final goal as the Hibees saw off Dunfermline Athletic to claim the trophy. This would be the only time either player would feature in this journey as Robertson didn't play at international level for another 19 months in his three-cap career, whilst Wright never played for his country again.

Another unfamiliar name in the starting line-up was goalkeeper Henry Smith, whose only previous international appearance came in Saudi Arabia four years earlier as a second-half substitute for Jim Leighton in a 2-2 draw. With one goalkeeper's spot in the squad up for grabs, this was an opportunity for Smith, who was having an excellent season for a Hearts side that led the Premier Division for much of the 1991/92 season before Rangers took control, to prove that he was an able deputy to Andy Goram in Sweden.

In midfield, Gordon Strachan captained the side and was joined by fellow Leeds United team-mate Gary McAllister. Brian McClair, who was predominantly playing up front for Manchester United at the time, was also deployed in midfield, a role he'd get used to playing for the national team as this story unfolds, and the middle of the park was completed with Maurice Malpas. A natural defender who played left-back or occasionally at centre-back, Malpas was asked to play a holding midfield position, normally occupied by Stuart McCall who was missing through injury, to give protection to the back four.

> Scotland: Smith, McKimmie (Durie 46),
> D Robertson, McPherson, Gough, Malpas,
> Strachan, McClair (Collins 66), McCoist
> (Gallacher 46), McAllister, Wright (J
> Robertson 76)

A paltry crowd of just 13,650 turned up at a national stadium that was beginning phase one of its redevelopment, with the west stand gradually introducing seats to replace the old terracing as recommended by the Taylor Report. Those few allowed into that stand got a good view of the only goal of the game, scored on 11 minutes, when a McAllister corner was flicked on by McPherson for McCoist to nod home from a couple of yards.

Before that, Wright showed a glimpse of what he could do by going down the right flank and playing the ball across for McCoist, who was ready to volley towards goal until a last-gasp tackle by Mal Donaghy thwarted him. The other real chance of note from a Scotland perspective was when Strachan robbed the ball off Michael Hughes in the right-back area and played it into the centre circle, and it was then brilliantly flicked by substitute Gordon Durie to release fellow substitute Kevin Gallacher. The Coventry striker bore down on goal, but goalkeeper Tommy Wright spread himself well to make a smart save and keep the visitors in the game.

At the other end, Smith was only called into serious action once, when Hughes ran across the pitch from left to right, cut back on to his favoured left foot and sent a low shot towards the bottom left-hand corner of the goal, which Smith spilled wide of the post. Other than that, the Hearts stopper had little to do as he eased towards a clean sheet and Scotland comfortably saw out the 1-0 victory. It wasn't pretty or eventful, but it was a win to boost the confidence and form going into the Euros.

Five weeks later, on 25 March, it was the turn of the Finns to visit Hampden. It was another mixture of experienced professionals and fringe players who made up the starting line-up, though there was room for one debutant. Dave Bowman had been a consistent performer in Jim McLean's Dundee United side for a few seasons and must've thought that the opportunity had passed him by to play for his country. However, just over two weeks on from his 28th birthday, he was given the best possible present by earning his first Scotland cap in a midfield that also contained Celtic duo Paul McStay and John Collins. Rather surprisingly, this was Collins's last involvement in this story as he didn't go to the finals, though his time would come as he played a prominent role in Scotland qualifying for Euro '96 and the France '98 World Cup.

The only man who retained his position in midfield from the Northern Ireland game was Strachan, who was making his 50th appearance for Scotland, thus putting himself into the SFA Hall of Fame. Unfortunately, it would be the last time that Strachan would represent his country as a long-term back injury forced him into international retirement before the finals at the age of 35. Andy Goram returned in goal behind a back four of McKimmie, McPherson,

Malpas and the returning Tom Boyd, whilst John
Robertson and Gordon Durie led the attack.

> Scotland: Goram, McKimmie, Boyd,
> Bowman, McPherson, Malpas, Strachan
> (McAllister 65), McStay, J Robertson
> (McCoist 54), Collins, Durie

An even smaller crowd of 9,275 turned up at Hampden
to see the last home match before the finals. Scotland
started brightly and took the lead on 22 minutes, when
Bowman took on three Finnish players before pulling
the ball back perfectly for McStay to drill home from
just inside the penalty area. It was a moment for
Bowman to savour as he looked to take advantage of
his opportunity to try and claim one of the remaining
spots in the squad for the Euros. This contribution
didn't go unnoticed by Roxburgh when he made his
final decision on who was making the plane to Sweden
in June.

The Tartan Army expected Scotland to build on
this, so they were stunned when Finland equalised
on 41 minutes as Jari Litmanen's fine volley nestled
into the corner of Goram's net. Litmanen would go
on to have a great career with Ajax, where he won the
Champions League in 1995, Barcelona and Liverpool,
amongst others. There were no further goals in an

evenly contested game and a 1-1 draw was a fair result. It would also be the last time that Scotland would play at the national stadium for two years as the Hampden renovation, which saw the north and east stands both get a roof and seats in line with the Taylor Report, meant the team were relocated during the World Cup qualifying campaign for USA '94.

If the two friendlies were uneventful, Scotland under-21s' quarter-final second leg of their European Championship against Germany was the polar opposite. Having earned a credible 1-1 draw away from home, Craig Brown's young guns were trailing 3-1 at Pittodrie before an amazing comeback earned a 4-3 win on the night and a 5-4 victory on aggregate to advance to the semi-finals. Not only did nine of the 13 (including two substitutes) who were on the pitch that night go on to win full international honours but three of them would be named in Roxburgh's initial Euro'92 squad. The report card from his right-hand man must've been glowing, but it also showed the attention to detail paid by the Scotland manager to the emerging talent who he believed could come into the full squad and make an impact.

It would be another six weeks before Andy Roxburgh would see his squad. All he could do now was keep tabs on his players' form and pray that his star men wouldn't pick up any injuries between now and May.

The next time he would see his squad, he would have his players for six weeks!

North American getaway

WITH 1991/92 being a European Championship year, footballing authorities across the globe were tasked with ensuring an earlier end to their seasons in order for players to be fresh for the big event. The domestic football season in the UK ended on 9 May with the national cup finals in England and Scotland, whilst the European Cup Final (for you younger readers, this was the competition that is now known as the Champions League, and only contained the defending champions of Europe and the domestic leagues) between Barcelona and Sampdoria at Wembley was played on 20 May.

In the modern era, that sounds incredibly early when you consider that the domestic seasons nowadays don't finish until much later in the month. For example, the 2020/21 Scottish Cup Final between St Johnstone and Hibernian was played on 22 May

2021, and the Champions League Final between Manchester City and Chelsea (second and fourth in the 2019/20 English Premier League campaign to qualify for Europe's premier competition) was played a week later. And this was the governing bodies taking into account the delayed Euro 2020 finals that kicked off on 11 June 2021. Although, to cut the SFA, UEFA and co. some slack, they also had to factor the effects of the coronavirus pandemic into their scheduling, including later starts to the season in some nations.

The fact Andy Roxburgh was able to have his squad five weeks before the finals in Sweden was a privilege that he ensured he wouldn't waste. His attention to detail was high and he had best-laid plans that were a good mix of intense training, useful match practice and enough activities during the rest and recuperation periods that meant his squad were never bored.

All of this meant that his squad had to have the best of facilities available, so a trip to North America to face the USA in Denver and Canada in Toronto was arranged for the first part of the pre-tournament plans. Once they flew home, there would be two days' rest to catch up with their families before meeting at the luxurious Dunkeld Hotel in Perthshire, with training at St Johnstone's McDiarmid Park, where they would be until they departed for Sweden. In between times at Dunkeld and jetting off for the Euros, there would be one more friendly, against Norway in Oslo, to familiarise themselves with Scandinavia.

Before setting off to North America, Roxburgh had the small matter of naming his 21-man squad for the tour. His plans were dealt a massive blow as Leeds United skipper Gordon Strachan prematurely announced his international retirement through an ongoing back injury. Fresh from leading the Elland Road side to the old First Division title before that summer's formation of the Premier League, Strachan was hoping to add a European Championship finals to the two World Cups he played in at Spain '82 and Mexico '86 but made the agonising decision to curtail his Scotland career after 50 caps.

Speaking to the *Daily Record* on 5 May 1992, Strachan said of his decision, 'This is something I've suffered on and off for about eight years. It comes and goes, but it's never been as bad as this season. It's like a shooting pain down my leg. With our schedule being so demanding, I've not been able to recover properly. I've been playing under stress since Christmas, playing for Leeds' sake, and I've been monitored all the time. What I did not expect was to be told to rest for so long. I was not even fit enough to play the whole game on Saturday [Leeds 1-0 victory over Norwich on the final day of the 1991/92 season], but the boss allowed me to play for the 15 minutes. That was simply to say thank you to the Leeds fans. I'm just sorry I won't be able to do that for the Scotland fans.'

Getting back into the international fold after an 18-month absence, which also saw him miss out on the Italia '90 squad, had made Strachan even more determined to play in the Euros. That's what made missing out on the finals even more disappointing, having played a prominent part in the qualifying matches to get us there. He continued in his interview with the *Daily Record*, 'Two years ago, I didn't think I'd any chance of a return, then Andy Roxburgh brought me back, made me captain, and it looked as though I would play against the Dutch and the Germans. Now, because of this back problem, that dream has ended. Quite honestly, it was not my decision. The doctors said the only answer was rest.'

Losing Strachan was clearly a blow to Andy Roxburgh's plans for the finals, but he could still call upon an experienced squad at club and international level to rely on in Sweden. Strachan's club team-mate Gary McAllister also had a league title winner's medal to boast about and was more than ready to make a midfield spot his own in the dark blue of Scotland. Brian McClair had a solid season at Manchester United, where he'd scored the winning goal in the League Cup Final, and his goals had United top of the table for long spells before their title challenge collapsed at the end. Also, in England's top flight, Gordon Durie had settled into life at Tottenham and had played a key role in Scotland's qualification.

Another man who made the cut was Everton's Pat Nevin, something that wasn't looking promising several months before. A fall out with manager Howard Kendall and losing his place in the starting line-up at Goodison saw Nevin go on loan to Tranmere Rovers, then in the English Second Division (or, as it's known today, the Championship) in March 1992, which became permanent in the summer. He rediscovered his form within those two months, which was enough to convince Roxburgh to gamble on taking him to Sweden. Even though he hadn't played for Scotland for a year (the qualifying match in San Marino, where he won a penalty minutes after coming on as a second-half substitute), Roxburgh knew that Nevin could offer something different to the group, with his trickery being a valuable option to have in tight games.

Recalling his somewhat surprise selection, Nevin said, 'It was brilliant to get in that squad, because I was right on the edge of getting in. I'd fallen out of the Everton team. I'd fallen out with the manager, more importantly. And, because of that, I had to go to Tranmere to get myself fit, and Roxy had said to me, "You need to be playing. I need to come and see you playing." He came to see me play and I was at the best period of my career, playing-wise, which was annoying not to be getting a game every week at Everton, but that's the way football is sometimes. So I went to Tranmere for a couple of months, Roxy came down to see me, saw that I hadn't lost anything – in fact, if anything, I was in great nick – so that's how I managed to get that last-chance hotel in going over to Canada and the US.'

North of the border, the Rangers quartet of Andy Goram, Richard Gough, Stuart McCall and Ally McCoist were all fresh from a double-winning season at Ibrox. Stewart McKimmie at Aberdeen, Dave McPherson at Hearts and Maurice Malpas at Dundee United were solid performers at their respective clubs and established at international level, whilst Paul McStay's Celtic form alerted clubs across the continent before he did a U-turn to remain at Parkhead.

There were a couple of surprises in Roxburgh's selection as three uncapped players were given the nod to join the party. Aberdeen right-back Stephen Wright, Hearts defender Alan McLaren and Dundee United's Duncan Ferguson had all impressed not only for their clubs but also for the Scotland under-21 side managed by Craig Brown as they reached the semi-final of their equivalent of the European Championship. This included a memorable quarter-final victory over Germany at Pittodrie as the side battled back from 3-1 down to claim a 4-3 triumph on the night, and 5-4 on aggregate, before losing 1-0 on aggregate to Sweden in the penultimate stage.

Bringing in the three youngsters was to expose them to what an international camp was like before a major tournament, and they'd also be handy squad players to call upon in the event of injury or suspension to the more senior pros. In addition, Ferguson's United team-mate Billy McKinlay, Aberdeen goalkeeper Michael Watt, Nottingham Forest's Scot Gemmill, son of Scotland legend Archie, and Motherwell's Phil O'Donnell, sadly no longer with us, were also brought along for the experience, though their roles were more to help out with training.

Unfortunately for Wright, his adventure was over before he could look out his passport after it emerged that he required an operation on a cracked bone in his wrist. It was a blow for Wright to have been pulled out so close to the tournament, and it turned out to be a *Sliding Doors* moment for him as only two caps were won the following year in a career that was ruined by a serious knee injury during the 1995/96 season. His place in the squad would go to Derek Whyte, who hadn't featured in the squad during qualification or the two friendly matches, and whose last Scotland cap was three years previously, against Chile in the Rous Cup. Whyte would go onto being called up at another two major international tournaments – Euro '96 in England and the France '98 World Cup – though he wouldn't feature at any of the three finals he went to.

Another man who had to pull out of the North American tour was Andy Goram, but this was more of a precautionary measure to wrap him in cotton wool for the Euros after having injections on a minor knee injury. Luckily, Roxburgh had named two backup goalkeepers in Henry Smith of Hearts, looking to add to his two Scotland caps, and Celtic stopper Gordon Marshall, who had yet to be capped by his country. The two men were vying for the role of understudy to Goram in Sweden, with the other to go on standby.

In between the experience and youth were a bunch of reliable players whom Roxburgh and Brown could call upon. The versatility and pace of Tom Boyd, now at Celtic, having had an unsuccessful spell at Chelsea, was a handy option to cover the back line and the left-wing position; Hearts striker John Robertson, whose early goals against Romania and Switzerland contributed hugely to qualification; and the dependable Dundee United duo of Jim McInally and Dave Bowman.

Bowman and McInally's inclusion took the Tannadice contingent to four, adding to the experience of their club captain Malpas and new kid on the block Ferguson. Their club manager, the late, great Jim McLean, was beaming with pride at seeing four of his players represent their country at a major finals. It was testament to the great work he had done to mould these players into the international set-up. He also made it clear to his players that this was an honour not to be taken for granted and insisted that they turned up for Scotland duty even if they weren't fully fit, so that the medical staff at the SFA could assess them.

Malpas summed up McLean's pride by saying, 'If you ever say to Jim McLean after a game that you had a knock or were struggling, he still sent you to the Scotland gathering. He never, ever wanted you to back out. He wanted you to play. He wanted you to represent Dundee United as an internationalist. Five players went to the World Cup in '86. He was keen for us to play. He was keen for us to be acknowledged. And we had four of us who were playing at United; Kevin (Gallacher) and Goughy had been there, and Jim McLean took an interest in how you'd done. After the Costa Rica game, I got a phone call in a hotel and he was criticising my defending because of the goal. As a team, we would show the player in the way. We never done that at Tannadice. We were the complete opposite: we showed everybody outside, and you were left to defend one-v-one or one of the centre-backs would come and help you.

'Andy Roxburgh had decided that was the best way, that the guys would show everybody in. I showed somebody in and they scored, and Jim McLean was on the phone complaining – why did I show them in? So he definitely took an interest in his own players and he never said to me, and as far as I know he never said to anybody else, "I don't want you to go, because we've got a big game coming up." By that time, I was a right senior pro and you were used to playing twice a week. Guys of my era played twice a week constantly. That's the one thing I'll say compared to now, who play once a week. We were playing twice a week in cup games, European games, so you had plenty of games. All the international games, they used to rattle on to each other, and as long as you could keep a reasonable level of fitness, you just got on with it.'

There was one other big decision for Roxburgh to make that was caused by Strachan's absence – name a captain! Speculation arose as to who would take over the armband, and there were three immediate contenders for the role. Gough, Malpas and McStay were all captains at their respective clubs and had taken on the skipper's responsibility at some point during the qualifying campaign.

Gough was the one who got the nod to lead his nation out in Sweden, a truly proud moment for the Rangers skipper who had led his club side to double glory. The move came as a surprise to some sections in the media as Gough didn't have the best of relationships with Roxburgh, but that did not deter the manager from picking who he believed was the best man for the job. In an interview with the *Daily Record* reflecting on his decision, Roxburgh said, 'I don't like yes men and have none around me. I would hate to have people agreeing with me all the time. Craig Brown, my assistant, certainly doesn't do this. There may be times when Richard and I disagree in the future, but it will be for the right reasons.'

For Gough, being asked to lead his country in a major tournament was a special honour, particularly as this one was being played in the land of his birth. Born in Stockholm in 1962, where his mother originates from, and growing up in Johannesburg, South Africa, Gough's story is an interesting one and some would be forgiven for wondering how passionate he really was about the Scotland men's national team, having had this upbringing. However, when I spoke to him for this book, he revealed that his father's passion for his country never left him when he lived in Sweden and South Africa, and that passion rubbed off on Gough when it came to international level.

Asked if he considered representing the nation he was born in, Gough replied, 'No, it was always going to be Scotland! My father was Scottish, and a very proud

Scotsman at that. You normally find the Scots who go and live in Australia or South Africa, like my dad did, or America, they become more Scottish than the ones in Scotland. It's one of those when they're away from home, so they're reminiscing about Scotland all the time. And my dad being a football player at a decent level, I was brought up very Scottish. Jim McLean and Walter Smith thought I had a chance of doing well, and they got Jock Stein to get me signed up for the under-21s as quick as possible. So I made my debut for the under-21s in about '81, so it was quite early, but I was always going to play for Scotland if I had the opportunity to do it, and I was happy I did.'

Clearly, representing Scotland meant the world to Richard Gough, so it's no surprise that he was also honoured to captain his country as well. What was a surprise to him was that he was chosen to lead the Scots in Sweden, given his difficult relationship with Roxburgh, and that he also wondered if the opportunity had passed him by six years earlier, when Roxburgh landed the manager's job. Recalling the moment that he was given the captaincy for the finals, Gough said, 'Andy Roxburgh wanted a private meeting with me, and he informed me that he wanted me as his captain. I was very proud to be a Scottish captain for the tournament. To be honest, I was a little bit surprised, because we had a few fallings-out with each other, like after the Switzerland game when I wasn't happy and he said he was misquoted or something. That was all swept under the carpet and we just got on with it. To be fair, it wouldn't have made any difference, because I thought in 1986 when Andy took over, I was captain at Tottenham, and I thought that was the time to make me captain. But he made big Roy the captain of the national team then, so I thought that would be the ideal time to make me captain. I was not shocked but surprised, but I think he made a good choice.'

So the squad jetted off to North America for the first leg of the preparations for the European Championship. It was a welcome decision amongst the players, to jet off stateside then north to Canada in a move designed to relax the players away from the spotlight back home, though the media representatives who travelled with the party were made to feel welcome.

When I asked him why this tour was selected, Roxburgh replied, 'We decided to play away like that, first of all, to gel the team. It also meant that we would play hard, train hard in the games, but it would also give them time to relax, and I remember distinctly the boys on the golf course and things, and they were happy to do that. It was really to keep them match-fit, but at the same time to mentally relax them, and to gel the group together. The two games in America and Canada, where we won the two, were helpful in keeping the team in form and keep the momentum moving. In retrospect, the build-up was appropriate and helpful for us, because, as national team manager, you find out you only get them for two or three days. It's not a coaching job; it's about leadership, management. It's about gelling a group together quickly to try and win the next game, and therefore preparation for a tournament is a completely different thing. Suddenly you've got them for a couple of weeks, suddenly you've got the opportunity to work on some of the details. That was definitely useful to us, so I think we went to Sweden in reasonable condition.'

Roxburgh's choice proved to be popular for the players as they enjoyed the first leg of the tour in America, staying in Chicago and taking in local attractions like Hancock Tower, Willis Tower and attending a baseball game at Comiskey Park. Some of the lads also enjoyed going to the local golf course on their rest periods.

As you can imagine, spirits within the camp were high – literally, in some cases, as Stuart McCall explains, 'We went to the Willis Tower, which was the tallest building in the world at that point. Some of the lads went to baseball, some went to do shopping and some went just a walkabout, sightseeing. We went up it. We went right to the top and I think wee Robbo was there, Gary Mac, Coisty, Durie, the Goalie might've been there. There was a bar at the top and there happened to be eight cocktails on the menu, so we all decided to buy one each. They were horrendous. We had to do a draw out, and whoever got one had to down it in a one-er. I remember that I got lucky – I think I got like a Daiquiri or something. But there were some absolutely horrendous ones, and I remember coming down and some of the lads were worse for wear, so I remember that part of it.'

Whilst the trip was popular, it wasn't without its issues as well, as injury problems followed the squad on tour. An ongoing hernia problem to Robertson caused him to be sent home after just one training session, with a final decision to be made on him going to the finals once the squad met back at Dunkeld in a couple of weeks' time. The last thing Robbo needed was a media frenzy at Glasgow Airport for his sudden departure from America, assuming the worst and preparing their 'sent home in disgrace' stories. As it turned out, the public relations department at the Scottish Football Association had failed to pass on the message to the press about Robertson's injury, before Roxburgh clarified the position at a press conference. This was not the first time, or indeed the last, where miscommunication from the SFA had led to the media making a mountain out of a molehill, though some cynics would argue that our journalists don't need much encouragement.

Robertson revealed the extent of the injury, and the 'Glasgow welcome' he received, in his autobiography, *Robbo: My Autobiography*, published in 2021. He said: 'All seemed well as we arrived in Chicago, and then right at the end of our first training session I felt an uncomfortable pain just above my right groin. Once the SFA physio and doctor had looked at it, they said that with three games in seven days it was best to send me back to Tynecastle to receive more treatment rather than just sit about getting treatment there, particularly as the squad would be flying to Canada as well. It seemed the right way forward, so I was flown back overnight to Glasgow, but was unprepared for the "welcome" I would receive. On touching down, I was met by dozens of photographers, journalists and TV cameras as they wanted to know why I was suddenly sent home from the squad. In their haste to get me back, the SFA PR team had failed to tell anyone that I was returning for treatment. When they found out a player was heading home, they assumed I had broken a disciplinary rule or something along those lines and that I had been sent home in disgrace. Fortunately, Bill McMurdo was there as I had asked him to pick me up and drive me through to Edinburgh, but we were shadowed all the way home by press. One photographer even decided to climb over my back fence to get a photo of the "shamed" Scotland player. Thankfully, Andy Roxburgh then told everyone at his press conference before the USA game that I was injured and would be receiving intensive treatment ahead of assembling with the squad before we departed for the tournament.'

Meanwhile, another striker was causing the management team havoc for different reasons. Duncan Ferguson was an emerging talent and had shown enough to earn a surprise call-up to the senior squad for the finals, but he tested the patience of Roxburgh and Brown on a few occasions with his somewhat lax approach, something the management team weren't used to dealing with too often. In his autobiography, *The Accidental Footballer*, Pat Nevin recalls such an occasion, when Ferguson wandered off the training pitch to chat to a couple of local girls, such was his disinterest in that day's training session. He said, 'Andy Roxburgh and his then-assistant Craig Brown were sticklers for everything being just so, spick and span and all in order. From players training hard to making sure your socks were smartly pulled up, things had to be done right. This negligent approach from the big man just would not do at all – his shirt wasn't even tucked in! The problem was that this attitude had never been encountered by either coach at international level, so there was a dilemma for a few moments while they considered what to say.

'Before they could figure it out, Duncan just sauntered off to the side and sat in the small stand talking to a couple of very bonny-looking local student girls. Roxy and Broon, as they were affectionately known, were aghast. From about 50 yards away, they shouted to him, "What's going on, Duncan?" Big Dunc didn't even deign to stop his conversation; in fact he seemed surprised and slightly annoyed by the intrusion. Instead, he held out a hand in their general direction and without turning away from the girls he shouted, "Ach, sair tae (sore toe)," and carried on with the chat to his "lassies".'

Ferguson's club team-mate Jim McInally was entrusted with the responsibility of looking after the youngster on tour by being his room-mate. However, when I asked him what kind of role model he was to Big Dunc, McInally admitted, 'I wasn't a very good one! I tried to be. I roomed with him in America, badly. I always remember when we were in America, we were leaving to go to the airport, and he still wasn't back in his room. Craig Brown, who was such a good guy, helped me bag up all his stuff to take it to the bus. The press were sitting on the bus and the hierarchy who was there at the time. And the big man – I don't know if he'd been with a bird or something like that

– comes in late. To be fair, I thought that was curtains for him, but he got away with it. I always remember one night, I'm sleeping, he's sleeping, and the hotels used to have a lamp in between you that was stuck to the wall, and he gets up and sticks the head in it! He was obviously dreaming and I thought, "Big man, what's going on in your head?" I loved big Fergie, but I failed him badly as a mentor. I did my best. He was one of these guys where going about with me was no good to him because I was too placid, so he'd far prefer being in the company of McCoist and Gough and boys like that. They used to wind him up constantly and get him to do stuff. They used to get him to take his top off and do 100 press-ups and stuff like that. He got a wee bit wheelied with them, but I just loved him. He was such a good boy underneath all they stupid things he done, and most of these things were when he had a drink in him. Jim McLean couldn't tame him, so what chance did I have of looking after him!'

There was, of course, a serious side to it as the squad trained at Illinois Benedict College to prepare for their opening tour game against the USA at the Mile High Stadium, Denver. The hosts were building towards the World Cup they were hosting in two years' time and were keen to show they had come a long way from the previous finals in Italy, where they were beaten in all three games. Soccer, as the

Americans like to call it, was still a bit of a novelty in the States, and it would be another four years before the creation of Major League Soccer.

With the Euros not far away, Roxburgh predominately went with experience from the start but also handed two players international debuts. Gordon Marshall was given the nod to go in goal in Goram's absence to earn his first cap, whilst Hearts youngster Alan McLaren, who'd impressed for the under-21 side, was given his first appearance in the seniors, alongside his club team-mate Dave McPherson in central defence. Stewart McKimmie and Maurice Malpas completed the back line in the full-back positions.

In midfield, Pat Nevin was given the chance to show why Roxburgh was right to bring him into the squad by being handed a starting berth in the right-midfield position, with the rest of the midfield being complete with skipper for the day Paul McStay, Gary McAllister and Stuart McCall. In attack, Brian McClair was picked alongside Ally McCoist, who had become the European Golden Boot winner, having netted an astonishing 34 league goals for the campaign.

Scotland: Marshall, McStay (McInally 68),
Malpas, McCoist (Bowman 77), McClair,
McPherson (Whyte 82), McKimmie, McCall,
McAllister, Nevin (Ferguson 50), McLaren

Note that the team is once again in numerical order, and you might be confused as to why McStay and McCoist are pencilled in higher up than usual. This is because the squad numbering for the tournament was now very much in play, and Roxburgh adopted a number-by-caps system to give players their number, except the two goalkeepers, who had numbers one and 12 respectively.

For instance, McStay was given number three as he had the highest number of caps in the squad behind Gough, whereas McPherson had McStay's preferred number eight jersey. More peculiar was McCoist having the number five jersey, more associated with a centre-half, and McKimmie had number nine, even though he wasn't renowned for his goalscoring prowess. Over an 18-year career in senior football, he'd scored ten goals – that included just one at international level – which didn't even equate to 30 per cent of McCoist's league goals in that season.

Speaking to the Scottish Football Forums Podcast, McKimmie said, 'I always get asked about that and I tried to explain that, other than the goalies, the caps you had for your country, that's how they did it. I don't know if it was to baffle the opposition or not. It certainly didn't do it. It doesn't matter what your number is, it's the opportunity to play on that stage at that level. It's just the kind of thing you dream about when you're a kid, that you'd love to play for your country. To actually do it, it's great and I'm honoured and lucky to have done it.'

When asked if McCoist gave him stick for taking his number and him getting a defender's number, McKimmie joked, 'He could never get up and down the park as quick as me! He's a great guy Ally, good at getting you in nightclubs for free. He's the kind of guy you'd love your daughter to take home with her and get married.' McPherson summed up the bemusement of getting the number eight jersey by saying, 'It was weird! You couldn't say, "I don't want that number." You were given and that's it. You were that number for a reason, which I never really agreed with. I played number ten once before, which is bizarre.'

To the players and fans, they may well have been puzzled as to why the numbering looked back to front, but there was logic behind Roxburgh's thinking, as journalist Hugh MacDonald explains, 'Craig Brown said to me, "Before tournaments, you have to get certain things straight, and there's certain things that can cause real disharmony in a squad, and numbers is one of them. If you've got two guys who want number nine, say McCoist and Gallacher, what do you do? Do you toss for it? Do you give it to one because he's going to start more? Suddenly you start having arguments about numbers, so we decided very early on that squad numbers would be decided by the number of caps, and if it came out daft numbers, fair enough. But it's better than the alternative, which is two guys arguing over a jersey." Now, to outsiders that might seem strange, but anybody who knows footballers, they put these things into contracts now. Football numbers stand for priority and a bit of ego as well. So I think that was a smart move by Roxburgh, it was the kind of thing that Roxburgh was smart at, just saying to himself, "Let's kill this problem by just saying that this is what we're doing. We're doing it this way," and then nobody can argue, because it's fair.'

In fairness, the squad didn't really argue, though they did have some banter with it. They had more important things on their minds than the numbers on their backs, including getting through the USA game without any fresh injury scares whilst maintaining some momentum ahead of the Euros.

Seven minutes in, Scotland got off to the perfect start. Nevin picked up the ball on the right wing and jinked inside before playing a neat one-two with McClair. The space then opened up and he beautifully hit the ball into the top right-hand corner with the outside of his right foot to give the visitors the lead.

You could say it was a goal worthy of a Hollywood movie. Well, this literally was the case as the goal was shown in the background in a scene during the movie

So I Married an Axe Murderer starring Mike Myers. Nevin takes up the story, 'I managed to score a decent goal, but most importantly, it is in a great movie. It's the funniest scene in the film. The film's brilliant anyway, but it's the funniest scene. It's the one where he's playing a Scotsman and he's shouting, "Heed, get out of the way." He's got a great Glasgow accent, and Heed's in the way of the telly, and on the telly there's a game on, Scotland against USA. Scotland score and he celebrates, and I thought, "That's me. I scored that goal." I went and seen it in the cinema, I had no idea about it, and it's amazing how you're sitting in the cinema and then, "Wait a minute, that was me. What?" You don't actually see me scoring it but that's them celebrating that goal. It was a great moment.'

The rest of the match didn't resemble a good movie plot, and Nevin's game didn't have a happy ending as he came off after 50 minutes with what should've been, a tournament-threatening injury and was replaced by a third debutant in Duncan Ferguson. Following an X-ray, it was believed at the time to be nothing more than bruising, though eight weeks later, a few weeks after Euro '92 was over, another X-ray revealed that Nevin had been playing with a broken leg!

Fortunately for Nevin, he was able to get by and take his place in the squad that went to Sweden, much to his relief. He said, 'Unbeknown to me, I got a cracked fibula later on in the game. Big Duncan came on for me. It was only a few weeks away from the Euros. There was no way I was going to miss it. I didn't know it was cracked, but I know it was a helluva painful. X-ray showed nothing, so I went anyway, and the wildness of it is, I managed to play with a broken ankle. I couldn't kick the ball any more than about 30 yards! Nobody noticed. I could adapt my game. It's nice being able to hit a 40-, 50-, 60-yard pass, or put in corners with a bit of whip, which you can do. But if you can't do them through the pain, you've got to play tiki-taka or dribble. I kind of knew it was getting better every day, but it was taking a long time. It wasn't until after the Euros themselves that I discovered, after having another X-ray, that it showed up clear, a big crack across it. It's not uncommon to miss it, because the first X-ray has bruising and mush around it, but eight weeks later it was better for the new season. My one chance for the Euros and I was playing injured, but I'd done OK. The chances I got, I thought I'd done not too badly when I got on the pitch.'

Nevin wasn't the only one to suffer an injury scare to have him sweating over his Euros place. Jim McInally had been nursing a calf injury towards the end of the season but had covered it up when the squad met up before flying out to America. He then came on in the 68th minute in place of McStay and instantly feared that the injury would flare up again during the game. Luckily for him, there were no ill effects from his cameo role and he was able to retain his place in the finals squad.

Recalling the injury, McInally said, 'What happened was there was a get-together at McDiarmid Park, and I was really struggling with a calf injury and I bullshitted my way through the training sessions at McDiarmid Park. I was in agony, but I would never show it and just get through it. We then went to America. I again remember warming up at the side of the pitch thinking, "My calf is louping here." Then I get the call to go on, and I thought if this goes there's no way back for me. But again, I managed to play 20 minutes or something. I got through the game and I just felt as though I've got away with one, because we had a good result in America, it was seen as a good result and I done OK in the time I'd come on. When we'd come back, there was an announcement with the squad, but I still wasn't confident that I was going to make it. Andy Roxburgh, I don't know if it goes back to the under-18s or if we won the Euros as a youth team [in 1982], was quite loyal to people like myself. So when the squad was announced and I was in it, I was just so happy, because, between injury and just thinking I might not have made it, I feared the worst. To get picked in the squad was just brilliant.

See, just to be part of the build-up and to see these things at close quarters, for somebody like me it was just something that I didn't think I would see so I really enjoyed it.'

Nevin's Hollywood goal proved to be enough as Scotland started their tour with a 1-0 victory. Next up was a trip north to face Canada.

Again, it was the same routine of train hard, relax and do some sightseeing to attractions like Niagara Falls and the CN Tower before taking on the hosts at the Varsity Stadium. As expected, Roxburgh rung the changes to give more players the opportunity for match sharpness ahead of the finals, with five alterations to the starting line-up that beat the USA.

In goal, Henry Smith was given his third cap at the expense of Marshall, who would not play for his country again. Also coming into the starting line-up were Richard Gough, who resumed the role of captain, Gordon Durie, Tom Boyd and Duncan Ferguson, with McKimmie, Malpas, McClair and the injured Nevin making way. Alan McLaren, earning his second cap, was moved to right-back in order to accommodate the return of Gough to partner McPherson in central defence.

Scotland: Smith, Gough, McStay, McCoist, Durie (Malpas 78), McPherson, McCall

(McKimmie 89), McAllister, Boyd,
McLaren, Ferguson (McClair 55)

The visitors took the lead on 23 minutes when
McAllister played a one-two with McStay, forced his
way past a defender before coolly slotting the ball past
Craig Forrest. Canada then equalised two minutes
from half-time when a cross from the right-hand side
made its way to John Catliff, who controlled the ball
well before lashing past Smith.

Scotland struggled to get past a tough Canadian
back line determined to get a draw, but eventually their
persistence paid off on 68 minutes. McAllister's drilled
free kick was fumbled by Forrest, and in pounced
McCoist to do what he did best by knocking home
the rebound from close range. With two minutes to
go, the Scots gave themselves an opportunity to seal
victory when substitute Malpas was brought down
inside the Canadian penalty area. McAllister took
the spot kick and hammered it into Forrest's top right-
hand corner to give Scotland a 3-1 victory to end their
North American tour in style.

The trip couldn't have gone much better, with
consecutive victories, no further injuries despite one
or two scares, and a relaxed atmosphere that allowed
a good blend of training and relaxation, taking into
account a long campaign, which included a 44-game

Scottish Premier Division season. Skipper Richard Gough was certainly grateful for the rest when it was on offer and gave full credit to Roxburgh for the way the trip was organised, saying, 'He was good to let the boys have a little bit of free time, and also, because it was the end of the season, we didn't do much training. It was a good squad actually. All the boys got on well with each other; they all knew each other well. There were a few newcomers, Duncan Ferguson being one of them. It was a good trip. We beat America 1-0, I played in the Canada game and I remember we beat them 3-1, so it was good.'

Once the squad landed back in Glasgow, Andy Roxburgh allowed the players a few days off to spend some quality time with their families before the tournament. When they reconvened, they stayed at the luxurious Dunkeld Hotel, Perth, whilst training at St Johnstone's McDiarmid Park. This proved to be a popular choice with the players as they had plenty of activities to keep themselves amused in between training, meetings and meal times. There was clay-pigeon shooting, a nine-hole golf course and a river for those who wanted to go fishing.

Bringing the players to a place with lots of things to keep them amused and relaxed was a smart move by Roxburgh, who appreciated that being away from friends and family would be harder if there was nothing for them to do during these long hours. This was not lost on Maurice Malpas, who acknowledged the relaxed atmosphere created by the management team, and he was happy to have a round or two of golf. He said, 'I disappeared and golfed. We disappeared up the Dunkeld nine-holer most afternoons and it was very relaxed. There was nothing rigid. You weren't really restricted. You had to be sensible – there was none of this going to the pub every night. You trained hard in the morning, and then in the afternoon the SFA, Andy and Craig would have things organised. Groups of us went shooting, have a shot of that, go to the fishing if you were into that and four of us went to the golf course and played nine holes of golf, and it passed the time. At night-time, we had the bingo and stuff like that, that was for a carry on, wind-ups, sing-songs, so it was very laid-back. I think Andy realised that we all had a hard season. It was a case that he wanted guys to be comfortable and enjoy the gatherings because it can get a bit boring getting up, going to training in the morning, going to your bed, getting up, going for a meeting, going for dinner, going for another meeting. It can get a bit monotonous, so there was plenty of things we were allowed to do. There was nothing regimental. It would've bored us to tears if it'd been regimental.'

Tom Boyd battles with Switzerland's Adrian Knup in the key game of Euro '92 qualification

RELIEF! Ally McCoist (grounded) celebrates his equaliser in Switzerland that proved key to Scotland's qualification

Ullevi Stadium, Gothenburg hosted Scotland's first ever European Championship finals match against reigning champions Netherlands

The first Scotland team to play at the European Championships

Battle of the number tens: Stuart McCall tussling with Netherlands skipper Ruud Gullit

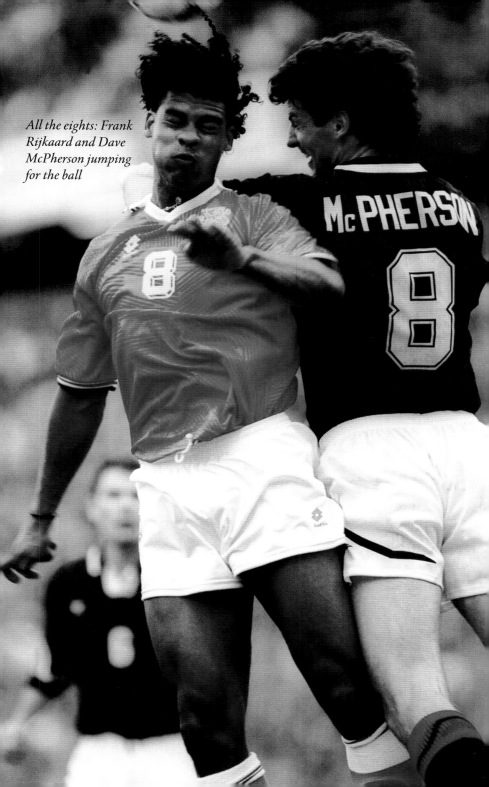

All the eights: Frank Rijkaard and Dave McPherson jumping for the ball

The Tartan Army had great fun in between games, and their exemplary behaviour didn't go unnoticed by UEFA

Brian McClair tries to get past Germany midfield enforcer Matthias Sammer

Fan Ally Wilson gets an autograph from Scotland captain Richard Gough

Fifteen-month-old Lynsey Brown takes in her first Scotland match on dad Jim's shoulders to see her side beat CIS 3-0

Pat Nevin (sporting the CIS shirt after swapping with Andrei Kanchelskis) acknowledging the fans post-match

Brian McClair is mobbed by delighted team-mates Stewart McKimmie, Richard Gough and Paul McStay after netting his first Scotland goal against CIS in the final game

Gary McAllister puts the icing on the cake by coolly slotting away his penalty to complete the 3-0 victory over CIS

A united front: Roxburgh and Gough put their differences to one side in Sweden, and the Tartan Army were right behind them

Another one who appreciated the activities at Dunkeld was Pat Nevin, a man with lots of hobbies. He particularly took to the clay-pigeon shooting and is seen on *The Squad: Euro '92 Behind the Scenes* documentary hitting his target with each shot that was captured by the camera operators, whilst others had no such luck. Although he personally was content whether doing clay-pigeon shooting or reading a book, Nevin acknowledged the importance of having so many activities to keep the squad amused during this time.

He said, 'I vaguely remember I didn't miss one! I was kind of the ace at that sort of thing. There was a lovely feel to the group. The dynamics, you build it by doing things that were entertaining and interesting, make sure people don't get bored. It wouldn't have been a problem for me, because I have lots of interests. I can sit and read a book for six weeks and I'd be happy, but it's not always the same for everybody else. Andy worked really hard at that. He was big on movies and all that sort of stuff. He'd really considered it a long time before anyone else ever did because he'd watched it before. You end up having fights in camps. You'd end up going stir-crazy, so he worked really hard on that. Our video man was the top man. He was just class because he was so friendly with everyone. There was also a good humour within the group. When you've got Coisty it helps, but there was enough people sparking off each other. You've got nice friends and a good dynamic. Roxy and Craig had rooted out the kind of people who might be, not bad influences, but not positive ones. That wasn't thought of before. Then, it was just getting the best players. It has to be something else. It has to be players sacrificing themselves for the group, and Roxburgh was very good at doing that. All that worked into it, and that's what gave us a chance.'

Whilst everyone was enjoying what Dunkeld had to offer, there was bad news for one of the contingent. John Robertson's groin injury flared up again towards the end of a training session at McDiarmid Park, and he then agonised over whether or not the injury was worth risking a place at the European Championship. After much deliberation, he made the tough call not to go to Sweden. Having missed out on the World Cup finals in Italy two years earlier, lightning struck twice for Robbo, with this one a particular blow, having played a prominent role in the opening two qualifying wins over Romania and Switzerland at Hampden. He never would get a chance to play for Scotland at a major international tournament.

When recalling making that agonising decision, in his autobiography Robertson said, 'As I cut inside and fired a shot from twenty yards, I felt that someone had stabbed me just above the groin. The whistle went and as we walked off, I knew then in my head that it didn't look good. I put some ice on it in the dressing room and, as we headed back to the hotel for lunch, Dave Bowman spoke to me, asking if I was alright, as I looked white as a sheet. I told him my injury had flared up and that I was going to have to withdraw, and he went quiet before saying to me "don't tell them, just go to the tournament as it's too big an opportunity to miss and it might settle down again." He was right when he said it looked like Jukey and Coisty would be starting the games, but I had a chance of coming off the bench and playing a part, so my injury would be okay for that short spell. He wasn't that far off the mark, but I told him I had a decision to make after lunch. I phoned Chris (John's brother), and like Bow, he asked if I could manage to sit tight and get through the tournament as the likelihood was I would be coming off the bench a couple of times. I got where they were coming from, but Chis also said I had to do what I felt was right and, having spoken to Alan Rae (Physiotherapist for Hearts at the time), I knew if it broke down, I was looking at eight weeks out with an operation and recovery and, if I needed surgery, then I would miss the start of the season with Hearts. In the end, I decided deep in my heart that I needed to do what I felt was right, return to get the op and be ready for the new season. I couldn't cheat my country and I couldn't cheat my club or myself. I was tearful as I spoke to Andy privately and told him that it had flared up at the last minute and that I would have to withdraw. He even got the doctors and physios to take another look after lunch but I knew it had torn. He then pulled a squad get together and announced that I was incredibly brave and honest and that I could've hidden it but had chosen not to. I was out and Kevin Gallacher was called in.'

As Robertson says, his misfortune was Kevin Gallacher's gain as he was now elevated into the final squad. Having missed out on Italia '90, Gallacher was delighted to be included in the party that would be going to Sweden, especially as he'd now settled into life down south at Coventry City and was reaping the benefits of playing in his natural striker's position. He said, 'I knew that by missing out on Italia '90, it fired me up and it made me even more determined. I settled in at Coventry, and the biggest influence ever was Terry Butcher. David Speedie had been going on at John Sillett to get me up as a striker and John Sillett wouldn't do it, and big Terry Butcher came down from Rangers to be player-manager. Having played against Terry a couple of seasons earlier, I was his first choice. He changed me and stuck me at centre-forward, and being the centre-forward changed me at Coventry City. I started adding goals to my game, and when I got those goals, people started talking about me in a different manner, and that's how it all changed. I was playing regularly, scoring goals regularly, so when '92 came around, selection was fantastic.'

The only other decision for Roxburgh to make in his final squad was who would be the backup keeper to Andy Goram – the choice being Henry Smith or Gordon Marshall. The Hearts stopper got the nod, with Marshall travelling as standby. Though, as fate transpired, both had earned the last of their combined four caps in North America. In Marshall's case, his clean sheet in the victory over the USA was his solitary appearance for his country.

So the 20-man squad for Scotland's first-ever appearance at a European Championship looked like this:

1. Andy Goram (Rangers)   Goalkeeper
2. Richard Gough (Rangers)   Defender
3. Paul McStay (Celtic)   Midfielder
4. Maurice Malpas (Dundee United)   Defender
5. Ally McCoist (Rangers)   Forward
6. Brian McClair (Manchester United) Midfielder/Forward
7. Gordon Durie (Tottenham Hotspur)   Forward
8. Dave McPherson (Hearts)   Defender
9. Stewart McKimmie (Aberdeen)   Defender
10. Stuart McCall (Rangers)   Midfielder
11. Gary McAllister (Leeds United)   Midfielder

12. Henry Smith (Hearts) — Goalkeeper
13. Pat Nevin (Everton) — Midfielder/Forward
14. Kevin Gallacher (Coventry City) — Forward
15. Tom Boyd (Celtic) — Defender
16. Jim McInally (Dundee United) — Midfielder
17. Derek Whyte (Celtic) — Defender
18. Dave Bowman (Dundee United) — Midfielder
19. Alan McLaren (Hearts) — Defender
20. Duncan Ferguson (Dundee United) — Forward

With the squad announcement made, the next worry for Roxburgh and his assistant, Craig Brown, was getting through the last friendly match away to Norway without any fresh injury concerns. Meanwhile, whilst Scotland were hoping for no disruptions from their final warm-up match, UEFA had to contend with a curveball to the finals themselves that saw a significant change to the Euro '92 line-up.

War had broken out in Yugoslavia in March 1992 after Bosnia and Herzegovina declared independence, following on from Croatia and Slovenia. The conflict forced UEFA to disqualify the Yugoslavs from the tournament, with their place going to the runners-up from Euro '92 qualifying Group 4, Denmark. In footballing terms, four nations would become independent – Croatia, Slovenia, Macedonia, and Bosnia and Herzegovina – and enter qualification for the Euro '96 finals, which earlier in the month had been awarded to England based on an eight-team format. The increase caused by the respective break-ups in the Soviet Union and Yugoslavia, plus the split in Czechoslovakia in January 1993 leading to the Czech Republic and Slovakia becoming independent, meant that those finals would be immediately increased to 16, now that 46 nations were due to take part in qualification.

Yugoslavia's ban would continue through to the Euro '96 finals, and they would next compete at the France '98 World Cup. They would then reach the Euro 2000 finals in the Netherlands and Belgium before they dissolved after their failure to reach the 2002 World Cup, being replaced by Serbia and Montenegro until 2006; those nations then entered separately going forward to the present day. Meanwhile, their replacements, Denmark, who were drafted in at 12 days' notice before the first game against England in Malmo, would go on to do quite well in the tournament, but more on that later.

Away from the chaos of Yugoslavia being kicked out of the finals and Denmark's players getting off their sunloungers to take their place, Scotland were in Oslo on 3 June 1992, for the last of their pre-tournament friendlies, to face Norway. Three changes were made to the side that won in Canada. Andy Goram was back in goal in place of Henry Smith after being rested from the North American tour, whilst Brian McClair came into attack in place of Duncan Ferguson.

The final change saw Maurice Malpas come in for Gordon Durie, with Tom Boyd moving from left-back into left-midfield. It was a milestone appearance for Malpas as he earned his 50th cap for his country, eight years after his international bow against France, and the occasion was marked with him wearing the captain's armband.

Reflecting on the occasion, Malpas said, 'Prior to going away, that was something you were saying – "Am I going to get my 50 caps?" There's plenty of things can happen: you can get injured at the start of training. To be fair to Andy, he took me aside and told me that I'd get my 50th cap, and Andy always said whoever was playing for their 50th cap would be captain that day.

'It was a proud moment for me to get to 50 caps, a milestone that got you into the Hall of Fame, that kind of thing. A young guy that played in a provincial team, you would never have thought that would happen. I'd captained the team before, but this was a big occasion, it was a friendly game, but it was still a big occasion for me.'

Scotland: Goram, Gough, McStay, Malpas (McKimmie 68), McCoist (Durie 46),

McClair (Gallacher 46), McPherson,
McCall, McAllister (McInally 68), Boyd,
McLaren

The game itself was a bit of a non-event. Other than a good save by Goram from Frank Strandli in a one-on-one situation in the first half, there was not much to write home about as the game petered out to a goalless draw. The most important thing, however, was that no injuries were picked up in Oslo, with the finals now just nine days away.

Malpas lasted 68 minutes on his landmark appearance before being replaced by Stewart McKimmie. For him, it was a case of getting through the game without picking up any unnecessary injuries ahead of the finals, knowing that he was a likely starter in Sweden. He said, 'When you get to that stage, the results are immaterial. We'd relaxed a wee bit, been to a couple of places, there was a bit of downtime, played some matches, trained, and we were getting nearer the tournament and Norway was the last game, so you were looking for a bit of sharpness, that was about it. You were praying you don't get injured; you don't get some idiot that's thumping into you. I've got to admit, guys like myself were virtually guaranteed a game if you were upright. I was at that stage in my career, I was one of the ones that was pencilled in, and if you turned up fit you got a game.'

With the finals on the horizon and Sweden one of the more expensive countries in Europe, not many of the Tartan Army ventured across to Oslo before the Swedish adventure. One of the few who decided to make the journey was Ronnie McDevitt, who saw the trip as one of convenience, with Sweden being a short hop across the water.

Recalling the trip, Ronnie said, 'Scotland played their last warm-up game in Norway on Wednesday June 3rd, which was nine days ahead of our opener in Gothenburg. It seemed straightforward enough to travel from one to the other and, as I was staying with my parents at the time and could work a fair amount of overtime, I was able to get £2,000 together to cover the trip. Before the days of budget airlines, the cost of a one-way airline ticket was pretty much the same as a return flight, so this required a return to Oslo for the journey home. At the time, Thomas Cook published an international railway timetable, which informed I could get a train early in the morning after the final in Gothenburg direct to Oslo for the midday flight. I booked return flights, paying cash through a local travel agent, from Aberdeen to Oslo on Sunday 31st May, returning four weeks later, on Saturday June 27th. The latest I could have flown would have been the Tuesday, but the Monday was a local bank holiday, so there was no need to take another precious day's leave and I decided to head out on the Sunday. I was alone in Oslo until match day, when I bumped into Robin Howat, whom I already knew. It turned out we were the only two travelling Scotland fans at the match due to the closeness and expected high prices in Sweden. The game was pretty poor and ended without either side scoring. It had seemed pretty pointless, but, with hindsight, it probably was a good idea to give the players a match, with only training scheduled thereafter before we took on the Dutch.'

The preparations were now done. Three wins and two draws from five friendly matches in the space of four months was decent form to take into the tournament, and the experimentation by introducing new and barely capped players was useful. It was now time for getting ready for the serious nature of the European Championship and proving that we belonged in this tournament, despite cynics saying otherwise.

Scotland's Swedish adventure was about to begin!

Baptism of fire

FRIDAY, 12 June 1992. The Scotland men's national team are about to step into uncharted territory by participating in their first-ever European Championship finals match.

They could not have asked for a much tougher start as they faced the defending champions, the Netherlands. Although the Dutch hadn't performed well at Italia '90, scraping through their group with three draws before going out to arch-rivals West Germany in the last 16, they boasted a talented squad full of world-class quality. At the back, they had Ronald Koeman, a great reader of the game who was also a free-kick specialist, as best demonstrated in the European Cup Final three weeks earlier, when his perfectly arrowed shot gave Barcelona a 1-0 win over Sampdoria at Wembley. Moving further up the park, you had the AC Milan trio of Frank Rijkaard,

Ruud Gullit and Marco van Basten. Rijkaard was the enforcer in the team, the guy who wouldn't shirk a tackle in the centre of the park when a battle was required, whilst skipper Gullit was the artist, a Ballon d'Or winner in 1987 whose skills gave defenders a nightmare. He also scored the opener in the Euro '88 Final against the Soviet Union with a powerful header as he led his team to glory. Up front, Van Basten was arguably the best striker in the world at the time. A lethal finisher who only needed half a yard inside the box to find the back of the net, Van Basten scored one of the tournament's most iconic goals in the final, four years previously, in Munich, with an outstanding volley from an acute angle to clinch victory over the Soviets. Not only did the trio play a prominent role in Milan winning that season's Serie A title, they also helped the *Rossoneri* to consecutive European Cup successes in 1989 and 1990, with Gullit and Van Basten each scoring a brace in the '89 final against Steaua Bucharest, and Rijkaard scoring the only goal in the '90 affair against Benfica.

If facing four European Cup-winning players wasn't hard enough, there was also an emerging talent whom Scotland had to pay close attention to. Dennis Bergkamp was the latest protégé from the Ajax youth system and helped the Amsterdam side to UEFA Cup glory that season. Now the 23-year-old, who was named after Denis Law, his parents' footballing idol, was ready to showcase his talents to a wider audience by partnering Van Basten in attack.

Five world-class players in one team – not much to fear, eh?

One man who wasn't scared of the opposition was Andy Roxburgh. The Scotland manager was embracing the prospect of pitting his wits against the world's best, and if he did have any fears, he hid them well as the relatively relaxed atmosphere amongst the camp carried on from the North American excursion and chilling at Dunkeld (away from training, of course).

The team made the relatively short flight from Glasgow to Gothenburg on 9 June, three days before their opening game, and the day before the tournament kicked off. They checked into the Sheraton Hotel and, the next morning, they trained at the Gunnilise Training Ground to prepare for the big game, before having a leisurely stroll in the city.

Stuart McCall turned 28 that day and his team-mates showed just what he meant to them – by throwing him into a fountain! To be fair, it was a hot day and his team-mates were just helping him to cool down. They made up for their prank by giving him a birthday cake whilst he was being interviewed on ITV by Gary Newbon, who rightly said that they were not that bad. It was certainly a birthday to remember for McCall, who said, 'I got looked after. I got drenched, and I got a cake because they felt sorry for me. Yeah, it was good fun.'

As McCall was literally soaking up Swedish culture, albeit not on his terms, Stockholm-born captain of the Scotland team, Richard Gough, took some time to catch up with his mother and some of her fellow Swedish relatives. Being a Swedish-born captain of the Scotland men's national team, he was of interest to the local media TV stations, who wanted to speak to the skipper, but he was caught off guard as they began interviewing him in the local dialect. At this point, Gough wished he'd learned to speak Swedish when he was growing up, and quickly blamed his mother for not teaching him the language. Even though he'd turned 30 that year, he still got a telling-off from his mum for that!

Recalling meeting up with his Swedish relatives, some of whom he'd met for the first time, Gough said, 'My mum had quite a few cousins there. My mum came down and I met her in Gothenburg. She'd come down from Stockholm, where she was living. She brought a crew with her, so I can remember meeting cousins that I hadn't met and I gave them tickets for the first games. One of the things she always reminds me of is that I got interviewed by the Swedish television for being not only captain of Rangers and Scotland but being born in Stockholm. When they interviewed me, they started talking Swedish to me and, obviously, I couldn't talk Swedish, and my mum says to me that I just blamed her for not teaching me Swedish. She was like, "How can you say that on national TV, blaming your mum for not teaching you Swedish." But that's how it was. I wish she had when I was a young person! When I go over now, they still talk about that, coming down and watching the games, so it was good.'

Meanwhile, Stuart McCall's 28th birthday wasn't the only big event of 10 June 1992. The ninth edition of the UEFA European Championship got underway that evening as hosts Sweden faced one of the pre-tournament favourites, France, in Stockholm. Jan Eriksson headed the Swedes in front, but a lethal finish from Jean-Pierre Papin earned the French a point.

The Scotland squad watched the game on a big screen fixed up by Brian Hendry, the video-analysis man within the SFA staff. Naturally, the players put on a few bets, such as first goal-scorer and so on, but they decided to go for more outrageous bets that were off the scale, even for the likes of Paddy Power and Bet365. Jim McInally takes up the story, 'My best memories were not so much nights we were playing but nights when we weren't playing. In the hotel, we had a floor to ourselves, and ITV and BBC were down below, where they had studios for interviews. There was loads of football, and wee Brian [Hendry] had the big screen, and we used to sit and watch games, but the biggest thing for the games was the betting before it. McCoist used to have the clipboard and used to be standing, and it was the first man to spit, the first one to pick his nose, apart from the obvious first goalscorer, red card and all that. It was all the stupid stuff. Some of the stuff he used to come out with was just hilarious, and we actually used to bet on stuff like that. Whatever was happening in the game, you always used to look for somebody doing something like that, scratch their balls, so it was constant laughs.'

Whilst the championship was getting underway, some of the Tartan Army were making their way into Sweden to cheer on their team in the tournament and have a bloody good time away from the stadiums. Some fans' journeys went smoother than others, though for John Wallace he was just happy that he and his mate made it to Gothenburg in one piece! On landing in the city, from Glasgow via Copenhagen, John believed he was heading for the trees and not the Ullevi Stadium.

He said, 'We flew out of Glasgow Airport on 10 June to Copenhagen Airport, had a few hours layover there, then on to another plane to Gothenburg. This was my first time flying and the approach to the airport was eventful! About 15 minutes from landing, we hit a thunderstorm! So I'm on edge. My friend's sleeping. The plane's started its descent and all I'm seeing is "forest 1000 feet, forest 800 feet, 600 feet closer forest" and my friend's still sleeping. This continued until we were just above the treetops; my face is welded to the window, looking for tarmac, so I decided to wake my mate up. He awakens to the sight of fir trees looking like they're licking the arse out of the plane. Then, out of nowhere, the runway appeared and the both of us breathed a sigh of relief!'

Poor John was still getting over the trauma of his flight by the time he joined the rest of the Tartan Army present in Gothenburg. As you can imagine, there was a good vibe amongst the supporters as they took in the local pubs and beer tents. Ronnie McDevitt was one of the earlier arrivals, having been one of the few who took in the friendly in Oslo before making the short journey across from Norway, and he gave a great insight into what the city of Gothenburg had to offer.

Reminiscing about his experience of the city, including turning down a ticket to see U2 because of prior commitments to meet friends, Ronnie said, 'There was a lively pub scene in Gothenburg during the tournament and, due to the number of such establishments, it was safe to assume this was generally the case. A large beer tent was open until the small hours for the duration of the Euros, which served pints of class-two lager in plastic glasses. There were three grades of different strengths of beer available, with class one the strongest. During that first visit to the tourist office, I had picked up a newspaper detailing the various attractions the city had to offer. I noticed a small ad for The Dubliner pub in a street called Kungsgatan and remember being rather intrigued. This sounds ridiculous today but it seemed a real novelty in Europe and deserved further investigation. I had come across a couple of dingy Irish bars tucked away down the back streets of Rome, but these were nothing special and the Irish pub explosion had yet to occur across the continent.

'Whilst Bono and the Edge were going through their repertoire in the Scandinavium, I located the establishment quite a way down the long road which eventually led to the docks. I met a few lads from Easterhouse that same evening who had arrived by ferry after concealing any sign of football colours as the shipping companies had a ban on all travelling supporters in place. This was not specific to the Euros and had been introduced following the Heysel Stadium riot several years earlier. In the days leading up to the Holland game, more and more Scots found their way to The Dubliner and we soon established it as our base. One of the barmen was from Glasgow, so we felt quite at home. The locals, too, made regular visits, with the bar able to accommodate large numbers. Often there was a queue for entry stretching down Kungsgatan, but the doormen were under instructions to allow Scottish fans priority. It wasn't a massive queue, maybe 50 yards or so, but a queue nonetheless. The funny thing was none of the waiting locals ever objected when we casually strolled to the front and walked in ahead of them.'

Despite the perception of alcohol prices being significantly higher, Ronnie revealed that beer was actually *cheaper* than the UK media were letting on, and that the beer tents opened later as the Euros got underway. He added, 'The Swedish government had reduced the tax on alcohol during the Euros, which meant a pint of beer in The Dubliner was around three pounds – around half of what had been reported in the media. The first couple of nights saw the pubs close around 1am, but once the football started, they were granted an extra couple of hours. Additionally, the beer tent served until around five in the morning, which was just about time for the first bus which headed in the direction of my accommodation.'

Ronnie may have discovered that some parts of Gothenburg had cheaper alcohol than others, but for friends Roy Brunton, Steven Gardner and John Morrison, who would later become part of the Beerhunters Tartan Army, they found a way of going to the matches without having to stay in Sweden. The trio – who, if you recall from Chapter Two, met in San Marino 13 months previously – decided to commute by Interrail, having bought a one-month pass each to use anywhere across mainland Europe. John had a collection of timetables in a book that was thicker than a bible, as he described to me.

Roy, Steven and John all flew to Paris with their partners and each would then do their own thing, predominantly, during the finals and throughout the month of June. In an era when mobile phones were a rare occurrence and the internet hadn't even been invented, let alone social media, the point of contact for keeping in touch with one another was John's mum, who must've been inundated with calls during this time. When I spoke to the guys, they explained that the plan was well thought out by John until the final part of their trip.

'Me and John met in Glasgow,' said Steven, 'and John had this book which had railway timetables of Europe, so John's basically organised the whole thing and, to be fair, only really fucked it up once towards the end. The girls were meeting us in France, and the only way we could communicate to our partners was by leaving a message through John's mum, and they would phone in as well. So we phoned in and we got a time wrong or something, so we're going to have to take a detour going up to Munich; we're going to have to go via Milan and Venice, and the message that went to the girls was, "The boys are having a great time, so they decided to go to Milan." By the time we got to Nice, where they were waiting for us, we got an absolute kicking for that, but it was the only one John got wrong.'

They might well have got justified grief from their partners, but it could've been a lot worse, as John pointed out when he replied, 'If I was going to get one wrong, I'm glad it was that one and not to miss a match or something.'

With some long train journeys planned, the lads needed something to help keep them contented for several hours until they reached their destinations. There were no smartphones or tablets to watch YouTube or Netflix via a 4G signal or wi-fi, and the trains didn't have screens in the cabins, so they bought themselves a karaoke machine to have a sing-song whenever they had a few beers, which was quite regularly, as you can imagine.

John recalls how much fun they had with the karaoke machine, and that Abba, funnily enough, happened to be the most popular tracks on the machine. He said, 'What was good fun, I don't know where we picked this up from, was a small karaoke machine, a handheld thing. We had international karaoke on every train – Germany, Poland, Denmark. That used to get us free drink and free food! We'd throw in a Scottish song if we could but it was mostly Abba, because everyone loved Abba because we were in Sweden. It was all fun and games on our side. I'm sure if we were travelling to work at 6am and you've got three guys with kilts and a karaoke machine in your face, you wouldn't be that happy, but we didn't see it that way.'

Roy added that the reputation of the Tartan Army worked in their favour amongst fellow passengers and train staff, which was in direct contrast to a number of England fans who were rioting throughout the tournament. He said, 'Everybody used to come and sit round us. We were the entertainment on the train! As the tournament went on and the Scots got more and more of a better reputation, we were stumbling, falling on trains with any sort of tartan on; it was like we were heroes. It was brilliant. England fans were wrecking the place. We met a few English lads who were trying to get away from it all. We had a night out with some of them in Copenhagen and they were nice lads, they were good guys. We felt sorry for them, because all they wanted to do was what we were doing, but they couldn't. Any time any of the English fans turned up, they ran riot. Some of the things we were maybe getting away with on these trains, if we'd been English, we'd have been lifted, to be honest!'

Ahead of the opener against the Dutch, the lads travelled from Paris to Amsterdam for an overnight stay before they headed for Sweden. Now if you thought poor John Wallace endured a nightmare journey to Gothenburg, the Beerhunter lads could step in and say "hold my beer" – for anything that could go wrong, did go wrong! Steven takes up the story.

'We booked flights to Paris. We'd agreed to get the Interrail because John organised this and we were going backwards and forwards. We got to Paris, we get on the train at Paris, we're going through Antwerp, you get shouted at for putting your feet on the seat and get taken off the train and have to come back on. We get to Amsterdam, and on our first night in Amsterdam, I get mugged by four big chaps and have my passport nicked, and John falls through a plate-glass window and ends up with 20 stitches in his elbow, arms and everywhere else. So, the second day, instead of enjoying the sights and sounds of Amsterdam, we all sat in a big park outside the British Embassy while I'm waiting for a passport and not knowing what the fuck had happened to John, because we had no mobile phones; we had no idea where the guy was! We kept checking in with his mum to say, "Have you heard from him?", and she started to panic because she's not heard from him either, and meanwhile he's doped to the gunnels in a hospital somewhere, getting stitches everywhere.'

What should've been a good night in Amsterdam turned into a disaster, which sounds a bit like the Euro 2004 play-off match when the Dutch smashed Scotland 6-0 after we took a 1-0 lead from the first leg at Hampden. Nonetheless, everyone was OK, and Roy, Steven and John carried on their adventures of Europe on their way to the game.

If you think the Beerhunter boys' trip was unconventional, step forward Grant Fisher! By accident rather than design, Grant boarded a supporters' bus organised by friend John Grigor that took in seven of the eight nations competing in the finals (the exception being Russia, or the CIS by their tournament guise). Talk about taking in the spirit of the finals! The journey took them the best part of two days. From your author's point of view, that puts a 20-hour bus journey from Cumbernauld to Amsterdam via Dover and Calais for, ironically, the Netherlands v Scotland in 2009 into perspective. What is it about this fixture and complex journeys?

Recalling that long bus journey, Grant said, 'John ran two buses. One left from Edinburgh for his east-coast boys and the other left from his hometown of Ayr. The plan was to drive to Dover, go to Calais, drive across northern Europe and enter Sweden from Denmark. All went well until one of the coaches broke down in northern Germany. We all had to disembark until a new one was found. Scheduled to arrive the day before the opening game, we didn't arrive until 5am of the day of the game. We got about four hours' sleep, then it was back on the bus so we could be in Gothenburg for early afternoon for the Dutch match. Our journey had taken over two days. We had travelled through seven of the eight countries competing in the tournament to get here. Missing only the Soviet Union. We started in Scotland, drove through England to get a ferry to France, then we drove across northern Europe, taking in the Netherlands and Germany, into Denmark and finally the ferry to Malmo in Sweden. Seven out of eight – not bad!'

Whilst the majority of the Tartan Army had arrived for the purpose of partying and going to watch their country play in a major tournament, another fan had an added reason to be in Sweden. Douglas Smith, originally from Airdrie but now residing in Essex, travelled with best man Eric to combine the finals with a second stag weekend, after the 'home leg' of his stagger back home in the UK. With Eric being at Italia '90, it gave Douglas the desire to see his country at an international tournament one day, and qualification for Euro '92 gave him an immediate opportunity.

Douglas said, 'As soon as we qualified, I said to Eric, my best man, we'll go to Sweden and, as it turned out, some of the guys from Airdrie were going to go to Sweden as well. It was basically me and Eric, but we did bump into others when we were out there. Because England had qualified, I couldn't fly direct from round here to Gothenburg. I actually went and stayed a night in Copenhagen the night before, and then got the train from Copenhagen to Gothenburg the day of the match and met Eric four or five hours before the first game. There was nothing planned, essentially. It was one of these adventures that we always go on, because you can never plan anything when you go and watch Scotland play; you just get carried away with whatever's going along.'

If some members of the Tartan Army were going through stress getting to Sweden, the team were pretty relaxed by contrast and went to do some more unwinding by going to a local theme park – which is very apt considering the Scotland men's national team have a long history of putting fans through a rollercoaster of emotions. By allowing the players to go to the theme park, Roxburgh was hoping it would settle any nerves they might've had before their opening game, and, judging footage from *The Squad: Euro '92 Behind the Scenes* video on the Scotland national team's YouTube channel, it looked as if the players had a great time and was another example of the 'train hard, relax afterwards' method working a treat.

The players weren't the only ones who were enjoying themselves in Sweden. Members of the Scottish media and their Dutch counterparts organised a football match of their own to take a break from their preparations for the real event the next day. Unfortunately for BBC Scotland commentator Jock Brown, who reluctantly played when the Scottish side had no goalkeeper, he suffered a freak injury in the game that threatened to end his role in the tournament. Luckily, he was able to carry out his role after being checked out by the local hospital, to the relief of his employers who would've found it difficult drafting in a replacement at the eleventh hour.

Recalling the incident that almost cost him the chance to commentate at Scotland's first-ever Euros, Jock said, 'It was the occasion of my last game of football. The day before the Scotland v Holland game, Scotland media played Dutch media – full works, the big park, that sort of thing. They said to me, "Are you going to play?" By that time, I was 46 or something like that, with a knackered knee, so I'm saying, "No, no, I'm well past playing, I can't play." I was saying no to playing, and then I discovered that the only thing they didn't have was a goalkeeper, so I said, "OK, I'll go in goal." So I played in goal in the Scotland v Holland media game, and the two centre-halves in front of me were Billy Bremner and Derek Johnstone. It was a right good game, taken very seriously; there was no messing about. We were attacking at one point. It broke down and they counter-attacked on us. Bremner and Johnstone were caught on the halfway line, the ball was played over the top of them and this boy with a bit of pace came flying through. He's one-on-one with me, I came out of my box. When I did play, I was centre-half, so my only thoughts were to behave like a centre-half. I actually put in a terrific tackle on the boy and I win the ball, but I go down on my right arm, and I'm knackered, completely knackered. Professor Stewart Hillis appeared out of nowhere and he says, "Your arm's broken. Come on, I've got to get you to hospital." So he takes me to this absolutely amazing hospital in Gothenburg. I end up with three different X-rays, with three different people looking at the X-rays, disagreeing whether it's broken or not. Stewart Hillis is going mad because he's saying, "I'm looking at all these facilities, and the clinicians haven't got a clue! In Glasgow, we've got the best clinicians in the world but no facilities!" Eventually, they concluded that it wasn't broken, it was badly staved, and the BBC went mental at me playing and getting injured, and I commentated with this arm strapped up. It was a right mess. So that was my last game of football!'

Andy Roxburgh was hoping that none of his players suffered the same fate as Jock that evening as they trained at the match venue – the Ullevi Stadium, Gothenburg. Famously, it was the venue for Aberdeen's 2-1 victory over Real Madrid in the European Cup Winners' Cup Final of 1983. It was also a familiar venue to three of the Dundee United contingent, Maurice Malpas, Jim McInally and Dave Bowman, who all played in the 1987 UEFA Cup Final first leg against IFK Gothenburg, which United lost 1-0 on the night on their way to a 2-1 aggregate defeat. The stadium was also host to another European Cup Winners' Cup Final two years previously, contested between Sampdoria and Anderlecht (which the Italians won 2-0), so it was proving to be a fairly popular venue to host big occasions. In terms of these Euros, the Ullevi would host all three of the Netherlands' group matches, one semi-final and the final itself. For Scotland, this was the last opportunity to do physical work ahead of their opening game of the tournament and the first-ever match played by the men's national team at a European Championship finals. After this, it was all about the mentality until kick-off.

After their final training session, it was back to the hotel to watch the second game in Euro '92 as England took on a Denmark side who'd entered the tournament at the last minute due to the expulsion of Yugoslavia. Having placed their bets on the outcome of the game and who the first nose-picker would be, they watched a game that had very few incidents to get anyone animated until the dying minutes, when John Jensen hit a shot that looked as though it was about to hit the net. At that precise moment, the screen cut off because someone within the watching party got so excited they accidentally knocked the plug out. It turned out they didn't miss a goal as Jensen's shot hit the post and the game petered out to a goalless draw.

The culprit happened to be none other than Scotland legend and joint record goalscorer Denis Law, who was a pundit for ITV's coverage of Euro '92. Who would've believed that the Lawman made the Scotland team miss the only highlight of a dull 0-0 draw? Recalling the unfortunate incident, McInally said, 'Something that I'll never forget because I worked near Aberdeen, we were watching England v Denmark, it wasn't long to go, and a Danish player had went through on the goalie, clipped it by the goalie, and then the screen went blank! We were like, "For fuck's sake, what's happened? What's going on here?" Denis Law comes running and he goes,

"Sorry, boys, I thought the ball had gone in the net and jumped up and pulled all the plugs out!" By the way, the ball didn't go in. We were obviously in knots. Because Denis hated the English team that much, he was so passionate about Scotland that he jumped up thinking Denmark were going to score, but he took all the power out of the place. That's a good story I remember about Denis Law because he was a hero, and you see somebody like him being so passionate so close up kind of meant a lot. We were sitting, because we had bets in and all the rest of it. Was the ball in or not? Well, we don't know because the screen's went blank.'

Denis may have pulled the plug, but the team were the ones who had to make sure they didn't trip up as they woke on the morning of the game. After breakfast, Andy Roxburgh held a team meeting to discuss the tactics for the game, and how to nullify the Dutch threat, which was shown on the documentary *The Squad: Euro '92 Behind the Scenes*. He then played a short video that listed some of Scotland's achievements – from the first television demonstration to oil from coal – which highlighted that even though we are a wee nation, we can achieve great things, and that his group were also capable of achieving great things if they believed. He also reminded them of just what they had achieved in getting to the Euros in the first place by saying, 'When you go out on that park, you'll be doing something that no other Scottish player has ever done, because there's nobody else who's ever played in a European Championship finals. All the stars in the past, nobody ever did what you're doing, and this goes for the other lads in the room if you finally get on during this championship. There will be something that nobody can ever take away from you. We not only have been instrumental in getting Scotland to the European finals but we can actually have an effect here. Wee Gordon [Strachan] phoned last night from Spain and he said to all of you, just to pass on the message, he said don't have any regrets.'

Next, it was on to the Ullevi Stadium to get ready for the enormous challenge of facing up to the European champions in our first-ever match at a European Championship finals. Fans back home were tuning into the game in hope more than expectation as they recognised the size of the task of facing up to Koeman, Gullit, Rijkaard, Van Basten and Bergkamp. Inside the stadium, there was a huge Tartan Army presence to cheer on Roxburgh's men, to inspire them to overcome the odds against their Dutch counterparts, whose fans were bedecked in a sea of orange in their section of the ground.

One of the many Scotland fans in Gothenburg that day was John Wallace. Like most, he spent a good few contented hours having a few beers with fellow Tartan Army foot soldiers, locals and rival Dutch fans, taking in the good vibe that had been created by the trip. There was a moment when two England fans wandered in for a pint, before they quickly realised that this wasn't a good idea with the stick they would get. John said, 'We assembled outside our hotel in Boras for our bus at around 11am, just under an hour to Gothenburg, where we were dropped off at a huge beer tent and we were in it until an hour and a half before kick-off. Dutch and Scots in the tent, the atmosphere was amazing and we were trading songs. The highlight was when two English supporters were going to the bar when their accent was clocked. In a second, both sets of fans spontaneously burst into a chorus of "if you hate the fucking English, clap your hands". The lads just turned about and left; it was hilarious. After an hour and a half, the bagpipes struck up and we marched to the Ullevi Stadium, down the tree-lined road. It was a beautiful day and the locals were amazing.'

After five months of preparations, the time for experimentation was over. Roxburgh named his most experienced side, numbered one to 11 in order of caps, after the goalkeeper, of course. Andy Goram took his place in goal, with skipper Richard Gough and Dave McPherson in front of him in central defence, whilst

Stewart McKimmie took up the right-back slot and Maurice Malpas taking his usual place at left-back. In midfield, Paul McStay and Stuart McCall would occupy the centre of the park, with Gary McAllister and Brian McClair deployed on the right and left sides respectively, though they would be encouraged to come infield regularly. Up front, European Golden Boot winner for season 1991/92, Ally McCoist, was partnered by Gordon Durie, with the latter being expected to help out if the midfield got overrun by the Netherlands' quality.

> Scotland: Goram, Gough, McStay, Malpas, McCoist (Gallacher 73), McClair (Ferguson 78), Durie, McPherson, McKimmie, McCall, McAllister

Finally, 22 months since the road to Sweden began on that wet September evening against Romania at Hampden, when there was apathy following a disappointing World Cup performance, Scotland entered the Ullevi Stadium to make their debut in the European Championship. Could they upset the odds and defeat the defending champions on their tournament bow?

The early signs were not promising as Gullit, being deployed on the right-hand side of midfield, gave Malpas a torrid time, skipping past the Scotland left-back on two or three occasions in the opening quarter of the game and whipping in some dangerous crosses that were repelled by Gough and McPherson. This was something that BBC Scotland commentator Jock Brown, who'd taken his place in the gantry after his own injury scare, noticed in particular. He said, 'What I remember about it was, in the first half, in the first 20 minutes or so, Holland opened up with Gullit at outside-right, and he was ripping Malpas to bits. He was flying past him and sending over cross after cross, and Gough and McPherson were fighting battles in the penalty box. Andy sorted it, but in the first half Malpas was badly exposed and Gullit was running riot. We didn't deserve to beat them, but we might've sneaked a draw.'

Malpas himself was only too aware of the battle he had with the Dutch number ten. Whilst the Dundee United skipper stopped short of saying that Gullit was the toughest opponent in his career, he realised very quickly that trying to get into a physical battle with the AC Milan star wasn't going to work. He said, 'I always remember, prior to the game, Andy Roxburgh was at me constantly that Gullit had been injured and he'd only got back to fitness, so you should make sure he gets a hefty tackle. I can remember early on in the game, he took a bad touch and I was like a charging bull. I hit him and bounced off him like a bit of fluff, and that was an eye-opener to me and I don't think I can intimidate him physically. Thankfully, he ran out of steam near the end of the game, but it was one of the things that you've got to try to see how you get on, but the physical intimidation was a no-no that day! I got a shock to my system when I bounced off him and I had to dust myself down. I was hoping it would be him who had to get back up and maybe not dust himself down. That was part and parcel of the game at that time. First five minutes, you could get a hard tackle, doesn't have to be necessarily fair, and get away with it, but that never worked that day. Initially, it was one of them ones where you think you're going to get a roasting. Thankfully, that never happened. I got it sorted out – well, the team got it sorted out, put it that way – and we were fine and played very well against Holland.'

Luckily, the Scots defended well enough to restrict their opponents to a couple of half-chances. One when Bergkamp had his back to goal and worked his way into a shooting position, but his effort trickled into Goram's hands. Bergkamp threatened again when his long-range shot deflected just wide of the post.

Having repelled the Dutch attack, Scotland then created arguably the best chance of the half, when Malpas's free kick was half headed clear by Gullit, and McStay then headed the ball back into the danger area and into the path of Dave McPherson. The big defender, who had a decent goalscoring record for a central defender at club level, controlled the ball well enough and was unmarked around ten yards from goal but dragged his shot wide of the left-hand post of Hans van Breukelen's goal with his weaker left foot.

Some cynics, including your author, wished that chance had fallen to someone more prolific, that is. McCoist or Durie, and not McPherson. However, there's no guarantee that either of them would've scored (remember McCoist missed two glorious chances four years later against Switzerland at Euro '96 before his beauty of a strike won the game), and credit has to go to the Hearts defender for being there in the first place. Recalling that moment in an interview we conducted for Scottish Football Forums Podcast, McPherson said, 'That's just what happens, but I've scored many a left-foot goal. You look back on it, probably a lot more composure, or if a forward was in that position, but at least I was in that position! Where were the forwards? I'll blame McCoist!'

The Netherlands then got back on the front foot and fashioned their best chance of the half, when a Rob Witschge corner found its way to Bryan Roy. His effort initially bounced off McCall before McStay lunged to stop his next attempt and the ball fell kindly for Gullit. He attempted to place the ball into the left-hand corner, but his effort went just wide, to the relief of a Scotland defence who were throwing their bodies on the line. Despite the onslaught of Dutch attacks, there wasn't a save of note for Andy Goram to make, other than when he had to stop a sliced attempted cross from Frank Rijkaard from sneaking in at his near post. A goalless first half frustrated the holders and Scotland could be content with their display.

Into the second half and Scotland continued to keep the Dutch at arm's length, with Van Basten being well marshalled by Gough and McPherson, who were forming a solid partnership in central defence. Although they weren't team-mates yet at club level, Gough had no qualms about being partnered with the Hearts captain and was good friends with 'Big Slim' off the pitch. Being partnered together for four of the five pre-tournament friendly matches would no doubt have helped, and their respective aerial advantages would be useful in both penalty areas. Describing their relationship, Gough explained, 'He was great. I got on well with him. I was always very friendly with him. That always helps, when you're friends off the field as well, and he had a good tournament. We were both good in the air and we caused problems to Holland when we did have any free kicks and we managed to pile into the box.'

Having continued to frustrate their opponents, the Scots then came closest to scoring in the opening quarter of an hour after the break when Van Breukelen was caught in no man's land from a McAllister corner. Gough then towered above Van Basten, who was helping defend the set play, but his header bounced into the side netting.

Nonetheless, the Scots were still more than holding their own and looking good to take a point from the European champions. However, with just 15 minutes to go, the Netherlands found the breakthrough.

Gullit picked the ball up on the right-hand channel and angled the ball towards the edge of the penalty area, where Van Basten flicked it on, Rijkaard knocked it down and Bergkamp sneaked in to prod the ball past Goram and into the net. A goal made in Milan and finished by a young man who was showing why he was regarded as one of the best prospects in world football. It was a cruel blow to the Scots, who'd put such great effort into the game. This was felt by Scotland supporters within the stadium, which is summed up well by Scotland fan Jim Brown, who said, 'I witnessed grit and determination from the Scottish players as we faced up against the Netherlands in the opening game. As the match played on, I started to feel that we were going to get something out of this. The team were knocking the ball about and looked like scoring and then, as is often the way, we were one down with 15 minutes to go from a Dennis Bergkamp goal.'

Douglas Smith, who'd arrived in Gothenburg that day for his stag weekend, had managed to get a ticket at the same end where John Hewitt scored Aberdeen's famous winner in the 1983 Cup Winners' Cup Final. Dejected at the late goal, he was quick to point the finger at a particular person who was at fault for the goal – himself! Moments before the goal, Douglas looked at the scoreboard and commented at how long Scotland had to hang on for a valuable point, only to be jinxed by Bergkamp's finish.

Ever since, Douglas has learned his lesson and swears that he has not made such a comment since in case lightning strikes twice. He said, 'When I walked in, we were behind the goal where Aberdeen scored the winner in the 1983 Cup Winners' Cup Final, in at the corner. We were only half a dozen steps from the front. The one thing I do remember, and it's not something I've ever done since that game because it jinxed us, was looking up and it said 76 minutes and I've thought, "We've got 14 minutes to hang on." I think it was something like the 78th minute they scored and I thought, "That's it, I'm never doing that again!" It seemed to drag on for about 20 minutes in the second half, and then all of a sudden the last 11 minutes went by quick as anything! Everybody was having a party afterwards. It's always the case with the Dutch, and some of them said, "We feel sorry for you. It should've been a draw." And we're all going, "Naw, you were battering us." But I'd need to see the videos to remember it.'

By the time of Bergkamp's goal, Europe's Golden Boot winner, Ally McCoist, had departed the field of play having endured a frustrating game, replaced by Kevin Gallacher. Roxburgh gambled by sending on his striking prospect Duncan Ferguson in place of Brian McClair to try and salvage a draw. The two substitutes combined when Gallacher nodded a long pass down into Ferguson's path just outside the area, but, being closed down, his shot sailed over the bar and the Dutch held on to collect the two points.

It was a good effort by Scotland against a team with at least five world-class players in their starting XI and who were amongst the favourites to defend their title. Scotland defended well for long spells, created a couple of openings of their own and, on another day, could've gained at least a draw, but for the intervention of the Milan trio and a young man named after one of Scotland's greatest players. Even the normally hard-to-please Scottish media couldn't criticise the performance that day, as journalist Hugh MacDonald explains, 'It was a really good performance that night.

It was very competitive, very enterprising, I thought. Maybe too enterprising against an absolutely top-class team. In no way outclassed, in no way shamed, and it takes a great player to beat us.'

Andy Roxburgh was certainly proud of his players' efforts in Gothenburg. He said, 'I think, up until Bergkamp snatches that late goal, we gave as good as we got in that game. I thought in the early part we were going to have a problem. Gullit was absolutely in top form, and he had an acceleration that was just unbelievable. I remember us quite quickly having to modify our set-up a little bit. Although we knew what we were going to face, they had so many possibilities coming at us, and then it settled down. We had some chances and I think we gave as good as we got. It was really an unlucky break that the big chance fell to Dennis Bergkamp and Dennis scored. All you can do at that moment is hold up your hand and say they had a bit of class, and that class won them the game.'

The Tartan Army appreciated the players' efforts and they, although disappointed with the outcome, were determined not to let defeat spoil their trip as they went for a few post-match drinks with their Dutch counterparts and some of the local natives. Swedes from most walks of life were happy to drink with their new friends from Scotland, including female solicitors, which was a pleasant surprise to

Kevin Donnelly and his friends. He said, 'After the Dutch game, we went to the beer tent and it was the first time in my life I'd come across a Portaloo, so that was a bit of an interesting concept. Got on great with the Dutch. There was a guy going around the beer tent and he'd made this banner essentially out of two small branches and big twigs. It was a reverse saltire, a white background with a blue cross, and in the white triangles he'd written "Elvis was a Scot" and in the middle of the saltire was a photo of Elvis that'd glued on to the flag. He was wandering round like some kind of evangelical creature saying the end is nigh, but he was saying Elvis is a Scot. We just had a great time. I remember we went to leave the beer tent and, as we're going out, I just said to my mates, "Why are we leaving?" because there was a string of beautiful Swedish women coming into this beer tent. So we went back into the beer tent, we got speaking to these four women, who were all very attractive, sort of late 20s, early 30s, and we said, "Alright, what do you do?" One of them went, "We're all solicitors!" We went, "What the fuck are you doing here? It's a football beer tent." I don't know if a lot happens in Gothenburg but they just said, "Ah, well, we thought that we'd just come down and party with the fans after we finished work," and you're thinking, four good-looking solicitors in Scotland are going to think, "Hey, let's go out to Hampden and that beer tent where there's all those football fans and we can party with them" – not in a million years!'

Whilst Kevin and his friends were chatting away to Swedish solicitors, Douglas Smith was enjoying the first night of the away leg of his stag weekend. Like most, he was enjoying a few beers with the locals, even exchanging shirts with a Swede at a nightclub. Although he was enjoying the hospitality that Gothenburg had to offer, he did feel the need to remind people that not all English people were as bad as the hooligans giving their country a bad name. The fact he was about to marry an English woman might've been a slight motivation for him to do so.

When I asked Douglas for his recollections of the first night of his stag weekend, he replied, 'First night in Gothenburg, I actually swapped my shirt for a Sweden shirt with a big guy from Sweden, so I do remember going out, but where we went and what we got up to, I can't remember! When I swapped shirts with this guy in the nightclub, Eric's seen the guy going away and said, "That guy will never get in yours." I'd put his on and it was down to my knees he was that tall – typical tall, blond Scandinavian – and he says, "He's going to wear that as a belt!" The guy came back to me and said, "Yeah, very tight, but I will keep it, don't worry. It's really good to have you in the country." He then added, "We're glad it's you and the Dutch that are here and not England," because of the hooligan side of it, and I said, "Well, they're not all like that. I'm going to marry an English girl. It's fine, they're OK, honest!" I think they embraced it all the same way that Scotland would do as well.'

A long Sweden top down to his knees was as close to a 'stag outfit' as Douglas would get, which might sum up how lightly his best man let him off in Sweden (although, we only have one side of the story). And there was generosity towards them when they bumped into some Scotland fans from Manchester, who offered them a lift to Norrkoping the next day, albeit they were so hungover they questioned if that had actually happened! Fortunately, a piece of paper confirmed this, and the stag and his best man were being transported across Sweden in a campervan.

One thing Douglas does regret was not keeping the names of the fellow supporters, who took only a bottle of vodka in return for their gesture, as neither he nor Eric heard from the Manchester-based Tartan Army boys ever again. He said, 'I remember bumping into three Scottish lads from Manchester who'd went by campervan, and they actually offered to drive me and Eric to Norrkoping the next day, so we didn't even use the train we'd bought. In the morning, we'd woke up saying, "Did we agree to go and meet these guys," and luckily enough they'd written something down on a piece of paper. I've always wished I'd kept this bit of paper to remember their names and things to get in contact with them, because we never met them again! We didn't even meet them after they dropped us at the hotel in Norrkoping, didn't even meet them in Norrkoping after that game, like hands across the water. All they wanted was a bottle of vodka and that was it. That's all they took. They didn't take petrol money, they didn't take anything off us.'

Not every Scotland fan stayed in Gothenburg to party with the Dutch or the locals, or even headed across to Norrkoping immediately afterwards. In the case of Beerhunter boys Roy, Steven and John, they had an overnight train to catch to go to Frankfurt before taking another unconventional route back to Sweden in time for the match with Germany.

Steven kicks off the story by saying, 'Because we had the Interrail tickets, we could come and go as we pleased. We booked overnights in the train and we had the cabins to ourselves, so that the seats folded in, and we done an overnight from Gothenburg. John had a friend in Frankfurt.' John then added, 'We travelled overnight from Gothenburg to Frankfurt, 16 hours. We had two pints with my friend and then we went back on the train and went up to Malmo, then across to Norrkoping on a beer ferry.'

This is then where Roy jumps in with the most important part of the story by saying, 'That's where we got our supplies!' Duty-free alcohol was definitely a more economical option than spending fortunes on expensive Swedish beer!

Meanwhile, the team were back at the hotel, minus two squad members who were forced to stay behind at the Ullevi Stadium to take a drugs test – McCoist and Stewart McKimmie. This was too good an opportunity to miss for team-mate Stuart McCall to play a trick or two whilst they were away, and get away with it as the blame was passed on to younger members of the party. He said, 'We left after Holland from Gothenburg and we went up to Norrkoping. I remember Coisty and Stewart McKimmie getting done for the drugs test after the game. We were having to get the bus to get the flight and we had to leave them in the end. They got a cab or a car and had to have a five-hour journey. I managed to get Coisty's key and did all these silly little pranks, opening all the salt and pepper and putting it in his bed, took the batteries out of the remote, cling film over the toilet seat for when he came in at night. He got home at four in the morning. The best part of it was we put it on to Billy McKinlay and someone else, maybe Gordon Durie, so McCoist and them were pranking each other and I kept chuckling to myself because it was me who'd done it, and I don't think he ever knew to this day.'

Well, if McCoist and McKimmie didn't know who the real culprit was behind the pranks, they certainly do now! This was another exercise in how close the group was, that they could have a laugh with each other and there be no fall out over it.

They were going to need all the team spirit possible for the next game. With the challenge of facing the European champions out of the way, it was now on to the small matter of the world champions.

From the frying pan into the fire

SCOTLAND WENT into their second match of Euro '92 knowing they needed at least a point to keep themselves in the tournament with one match remaining. If facing European champions the Netherlands was hard enough, the challenge was going to get even tougher as they faced up to world champions Germany in Norrkoping.

Despite their pedigree, the Germans were not in a great place going into the game. They lost to Wales in their qualifying campaign and only clinched first place in the final game, and had lost influential skipper Lothar Matthaus to injury for the finals. In the opening game against the CIS, they lost his successor to the armband, Rudi Voller, with a broken arm and were within a whisker of defeat before a last-minute Thomas Hassler free kick salvaged a 1-1 draw.

That said, this was still a Germany squad who were defending world champions and were fully expected to sweep the Scots aside and progress through to the semi-finals. Ten of the West German squad that conquered the world at Italia '90 were in Sweden, with Matthias Sammer from the East German contingent emerging as a top player. Germany were now managed by Berti Vogts, who won this tournament as a player 20 years previously, before adding the World Cup in his homeland two years later. Vogts succeeded the great Franz Beckenbauer as manager after assisting him for four years and was hoping that he could emulate the success he had during his 96-capped playing career. Of course, Vogts would go on to manage Scotland a decade later, but for now he was plotting their downfall.

The Scots had now moved from their Gothenburg surroundings into their new base at Villa Fridhem in Norrkoping, approximately 19 kilometres from the Idrottspark stadium. This was the smallest of the four venues in the tournament, with a capacity of just 19,414, smaller than Tynecastle, Easter Road and Pittodrie. When you consider that the smallest venue for last year's delayed Euro 2020 finals was Parken, Copenhagen, at just over 38,000, it really is a sign of the times that bigger venues are required for tournaments in the modern day, where more fans are able to travel more freely to these events and demand is high. Well, this was the case pre-Covid at least!

Although classified as a city, Norrkoping itself was not large, with a population of around 120,000 at the time, around a tenth of the population of Gothenburg. As you can imagine, there weren't too many bars for the Tartan Army to go for a few drinks and accommodation was sparse, which led to most people choosing to set base at local campsites.

The lack of accommodation caught out the well-travelled Kevin Donnelly, who'd been following Scotland home and away since the late 1970s. He revealed to me that he and his friends flew to Stockholm, then would sort out accommodation with a travel agent. When it came to sorting out where to stay in Norrkoping, he got a rude awakening as to how little was on offer, before being given two choices – a cabin hut in the woods or sleep in the streets!

Speaking of that experience, Kevin said, 'We ended up in a campsite outside of Gothenburg. Then we got to Norrkoping, we ended up in what can only be described as a "but and ben"-type place, ten kilometres out in the countryside. I'd been to Sweden before, been to Stockholm and Gothenburg before, never been to Norrkoping, but we thought, "We'll turn up in Norrkoping and we'll just get a hotel." Norrkoping is a glorified Forfar and they [travel agents] are just looking at us, going "nope". It was like, "If you don't take this sort of camping hut in the wild, then you'll be sleeping in the streets." We were completely naïve thinking we'd get a hotel or a hostel or something, and we ended up in this cabin in the woods!'

Whilst Kevin and his mates came to terms with the misfortune of being stuck in the woods, Douglas Smith could not have been more complimentary about Norrkoping. On his stag weekend, Douglas bumped into a few fellow Airdrieonians supporters he knew, and also had his first round of drinks bought, inadvertently, by Rod Stewart, who'd kindly left some money behind the bar for the Tartan Army to enjoy a few drinks on him.

It was turning into a great stagger for Douglas, who said, 'I loved Norrkoping. It was brilliant. Maybe because it was so small, we always seemed to bump into somebody. That's where we met the Airdrie guys, for instance, in the hotel we stayed in. There was a guy probably in his 60s at the time, and he was playing one of the Airdrie songs that I grew up with – "A Diamond for Me". The guy's sitting playing a guitar in the hotel as we came in to check in. The first bar I went to, it turned into a nightclub afterwards. There was an Irish folk band on, was a very long bar, and I went to the guy behind the bar to pay him, and he says, "No, it's OK, Rod

Stewart's been on singing with them and he's left money behind the bar." So the first round was on Rod Stewart. I always say that Rod Stewart bought me a drink on my stag weekend!'

Meanwhile, Scotland were preparing for their do-or-die clash with the world champions in their bid to prolong their stay beyond the group stages and give Rod another opportunity to buy drinks for his fellow supporters. Before the Scots and the Germans went head-to-head in the second round of fixtures in Group 2, there were two more fixtures played in Group 1 the previous evening. France and England played out a rather uneventful goalless draw in Malmo, whilst hosts Sweden defeated Scandinavian neighbours Denmark 1-0 thanks to a strike by Tomas Brolin, whose name would become popular with the Tartan Army later in the finals. Victory took the Swedes top of the group on three points, France and England both had two points from consecutive games, whilst the Danes sat in bottom spot as expected and required victory in their final game against the French to have any chance of progression.

The Scots had to avoid defeat if they wanted to keep themselves in the tournament, but realistically knew that they needed to beat the Germans to have any hope of reaching the semi-finals. Defeat and it was game over before the final round of fixtures.

Andy Roxburgh was determined to overcome the odds and keep Scotland's hopes of progression to the semi-finals alive. Unsurprisingly, he named the same starting XI that put in a brave performance against the Dutch in their opening game, trusting that those players were capable of producing a shock result.

Whilst it could be argued that the game against the Netherlands had an element of looking to hit the Dutch on the counter, the approach would be entirely different in a game we had to win – even if it was against the world champions. Explaining the mentality going into the game, Roxburgh said, 'We go into the game against Germany obviously under enormous pressure, because you can't afford to lose again. You've not only got to avoid losing but you've got to try and win the game, so that you put yourself back in business, and that was exactly our approach. A lot of people would now look at us, looking back on it, and say that we were naïve, but sometimes naïvety is also adventurous. People who are adventurous can be labelled as naïve if it doesn't work.

'Today, a lot of people would've said park the bus, play counter-attacking football, see if you can keep them at bay and see if you can snatch a goal. Now that might've been an approach that many people would've taken, but the approach and the mentality of our players wasn't to do that. They wanted to compete, and secondly, they wanted to go forward at every opportunity. We approached that game, we did not, at any point, decide to park the bus and defend. Our attitude to that game was "we're going to go out and win this", and we went out there and gave it everything.'

Scotland: Goram, Gough, McStay, Malpas, McCoist (Gallacher 68), McClair, Durie (Nevin 55), McPherson, McKimmie, McCall, McAllister

Germany lined up with six starters from the side that beat Argentina in the World Cup Final at Italia '90, indicating a statement of their intent to sweep the Scots aside. To the outside world, this result was a foregone conclusion.

Nobody had shown Scotland the script as they came charging at their opponents from the off, and it wasn't long before they got their first chance of the game. Richard Gough climbed above Jurgen Kohler to get his head on the end of a Gary McAllister free kick, only for Bodo Illgner to tip the ball over the bar.

This set the tone for the opening 20 minutes as Scotland took the game to their opponents. It's hard to believe in an era when teams like ourselves would normally set up with ten men behind the ball looking to counter-attack against elite opposition. Not the class of '92 – they had full belief in their ability to take on the Germans and created enough chances to at least go one in front.

Firstly, Paul McStay played a great reverse pass to McAllister, who'd made a run in behind the German defence. He was then thwarted by a good save by the onrushing Illgner, who'd come out to narrow the angle and deny the Leeds midfielder. The German number one was required again shortly afterwards, when Stuart McCall lofted a pass in behind the defence for Brian McClair. Again Illgner came off his line and got a touch on the ball as McClair tried to nick a shot over him. For McClair, who had hit 25 goals for Manchester United that season, he was still chasing that elusive first goal in his 25th appearance for his country, a statistic that frustrated many Scotland fans, considering his prolific form at Old Trafford.

McAllister had another go at goal after an attempted pass by McClair was headed away by Guido Buchwald into his path. He caught the ball beautifully on the volley, but his shot ended up just wide of Illgner's right-hand post. Moments later, he created Scotland's next, and possibly best, opportunity by sending a dangerous free kick into the back post. Dave McPherson sneaked in front of Jurgen Klinsmann but got his left foot under the ball from around five yards and his effort sailed into the crowd behind Illgner's goal.

With all of these opportunities going begging, you just had an inkling that this wasn't going to be Scotland's day. Kevin Donnelly, who was one of many Scotland fans there that day, could sense that we would get punished. He said, 'The Germany game, we battered them for the first 20 minutes. We absolutely battered them. I turned to my mates and said, "We might as well give up, because if we're not going to score after all this we're never going to score," and then they just go up the other end and score. You've got to take your chances when you apply pressure.'

After repelling the Scots for so long, Germany then began to assert themselves on the game and very nearly took the lead when Jurgen Klinsmann got his head on the end of a Thomas Hassler corner. His effort was brilliantly saved by the feet of Andy Goram before the ball was booted clear by McStay. Klinsmann then had another opportunity after some good play by Hassler, who got a half yard on McPherson before sending the ball across goal, only for the striker to miss the ball at the near post as he attempted to shoot for goal.

However, the pressure was building, and the inevitable happened on 29 minutes as the Germans took the lead with a very well-worked goal.

Andreas Moller played a pass into Matthias Sammer, who, with his back to goal, flicked the ball away from Stuart McCall and then laid it into Klinsmann. The striker used his upper-body strength brilliantly to hold off Gough, which allowed strike partner Karl-Heinz Riedle to lash the ball into the bottom right-hand corner of Goram's goal. Like in the opening game, it was a moment of quality from a top-class side that broke Scotland down, and that moment reminded everyone why Germany were the world champions.

Scotland went in at half-time a goal down but not disheartened, following a first-half performance that had everything but the most important thing in football – a goal. They had taken the game to Germany and had good reason to believe they could turn things around if they could repeat their performance of the first half.

What they needed to do more than anything was not lose a second goal, but two minutes into the second half, the nightmare scenario unfolded. If the opening goal came from a touch of class, the second was one of the most fortunate pieces of luck an opposition team has ever had against the Scotland men's national team.

Stefan Effenberg carried the ball down the right flank with Maurice Malpas jockeying him. He then attempted a cross that deflected off the left shin of

Malpas, looped over Goram, who slipped whilst back-pedalling, and into the corner of the net. It was the cruellest blow possible for Scotland and their task of salvaging anything from the game became monumental.

Recalling that moment, Malpas said, 'That summed up our luck in the tournament. Against Holland, we had a couple of chances but didn't get a break of the ball. That game against Germany was probably one of the best games that I'd played in, in terms of how the team played. If anybody had said you'll play against Germany, the world champions, and you'll get that number of attempts on goal, and you'll have a fair say in how the game's getting played, a lot of folk would lock you up if you said that. On the day, we controlled a lot of the game. Obviously we couldn't get the goal, but if somebody had been dropped from the moon, they'd be wondering who the world champions were and who were the run-of-the-mill team, and a lot of them would've got that wrong because that was one of Scotland's better games in terms of how they played. We created tons of chances, which is not one of the main assets of a Scotland team. In a game of three or four really good chances, you're hoping you get one. Against Germany, we created tons of chances and, unfortunately, we never got the goal. The deflection for their second goal was just a mind-boggling "how can that happen?" None of us could believe it. It catches the bottom of my shin guard, and it dipped inside the far post. It could've went any place. It would've been better if I'd missed it, but that summed us up then. We'd done all the work, all the pressing, and they've run up the park and scored. That kills the game.'

The Tartan Army were also cursing their luck as that freak goal occurred. Douglas Smith recalls how they were in good spirits going into the second half after seeing a pipe band on the pitch during the half-time interval, only to be put into stunned silence when that goal went in almost immediately after the restart. He said, 'The strangest emotion was there was a pipe band playing on the pitch at half-time and the Germans and locals were loving it. At the start of the second half, the pipe band came into the Scotland end. We were four or five rows from the front and they came in with us. Just as they went to start playing was when the ball looped over Goram's head into the corner. It was as if someone had taken a dagger to your hearts.'

Lesser sides would've thrown in the towel at this moment – not this team. Scotland came charging at the Germans again in a valiant attempt to get back into the game. Pat Nevin was introduced to the field of play in place of Gordon Durie, and he recalls his eagerness at getting an opportunity to test himself against the German wing-backs. Nevin said, 'I'm thinking, "Let me on! I'll do some damage here." I'd been watching this guy [Michael] Schulz [who came on as a substitute] at right-back, thinking, "I'm not sure they can defend." At left-back, [Andreas] Brehme's good going forward, but I'm thinking, "Let me at him." You want that creativity added, and I think in the second half we bombarded them for a bit. We got to the by-line a lot of times, got really dangerous crosses in, but the ball just wouldn't fall. Times where people like Coisty in the past always happened to be in the right place and the ball would fall for them, it wouldn't bleeding well fall for us! Had we got one, they were ready to crumble, and in hindsight you look at things differently, but I think we were very frustrated that we were going out and we feel we were better than that.'

Nevin's pace and trickery gave the Scots some injection and they began to take the game to the Germans again, beginning to create chances both from open play and set pieces. A free kick from McAllister presented the next opportunity for McClair who, from six yards out and unchallenged, headed the ball wide of the target.

As Scotland opened up more, they also became vulnerable on the counter-attack and Germany came agonisingly close on two occasions to putting the game beyond doubt. Firstly, Hassler ran through the middle of the park and laid the ball off to Andreas Moller, whose first-time shot cannoned off Goram's right-hand post. Next, Hassler carried the ball from the right-hand channel, moved into the space created by a clever run from Moller and unleashed a powerful left-foot shot that hit the left-hand post.

In between those let-offs, Illgner was called upon to preserve the Germans' two-goal advantage. From McAllister's corner, he beat away a Gough header, with McClair lurking, as far as McStay, whose powerful low shot was well held by the German number one. Gough's aerial ability was causing the Germany defence some trouble as he got his head on the end of another McAllister corner to knock the ball across goal. Both Ally McCoist and Nevin had opportunities from this knockdown, but their efforts were well blocked by the German defence.

Such was the pressure being applied by the Scots, Vogts felt the need to sacrifice Riedle for right-back Stefan Reuter, another World Cup winner, in a bid to repel the Scots' attack. Reuter would make unwanted Euros history by becoming the first substitute to be substituted as his ten-minute appearance was ended by a nasty head collision with Stuart McCall, who had gone in with the intent to head the ball for goal.

Although it was an obvious accident, Reuter didn't see it this way as he refused to acknowledge McCall's apology at the end of the match. McCall takes up the story, 'The abiding memory of that is they brought the boy Reuter on. The ball bounced and I've gone in and it's full-on. I've got a chance of scoring a goal here, and I've gone to head it in and he's gone to head it and the ball went into the air. It was a genuine attempt to win the ball and he was down, bandages, stretchered off. I remember Goughie doing the same with Buchwald. Goughie caught him on the back of the head, and he went off with a bandaged head. I remember at the end of the game, I went into their dressing room, one of the staff said, "He's just round the back." I went in and he must've had some stitches and he had his head bandaged, and he didn't want to know; he just blanked me and I thought, "You cheeky basket." I didn't need to go in, because it wasn't an over-the-top challenge. I didn't elbow him, I didn't punch him. It was a genuine attempt for the ball. I ended up with a bit of a sore head, but that was the beers later! Obviously, it was disappointing. I don't know if he ended up back playing in the tournament. I thought he might've accepted my apology. He just sort of waved me away, and I think it was the doctor who said, "I'm sorry, we appreciate you coming in," because I think everyone knew it was an accident.'

Reuter's cameo role certainty left an impression on the Scotland squad as they mocked him in training before the final game. Jim McInally, an unused substitute, recalls the then-Juventus full-back having such a poor game that any mistakes in training were named in his honour. He said, 'Reuter had a shocker and after that, whenever we trained and you done something wrong, we'd say, "You're having a fucking Reuter." Something ridiculous happened, and that was always something that stuck out, other than we were better than them, because he was with these guys and you think what a reputation this guy has got, and he was hopeless.'

Michael Schulz came on in place of Reuter, by which time Kevin Gallacher had replaced McCoist for the second consecutive game. Scotland continued to press for the goals they needed to keep their tournament hopes alive, but luck just wasn't on their side. This was summed up by a McAllister free kick that deflected off Guido Buchwald in the German wall, which wrong-footed Illgner but dipped just over the bar rather than into the net like Effenberg's deflected cross at the start of the second period. Buchwald would also be the unfortunate victim following an innocuous clash of heads with a Scotland player, this time with Richard Gough being the Scot involved. With both substitutions committed by the

Germans, Buchwald decided to allow the medical staff to bandage his head and carried on to help his team try to see the game out.

The fact Buchwald had a concussion and was allowed to carry on is something that would be frowned on in the modern day, and with some justification as players' health and safety becomes a bigger concern. Back in 1992, it wasn't even discussed. Buchwald was more understanding of the fact that the collision with Gough was totally accidental, unlike his frustrated team-mate. Gough was just surprised that he didn't get his usual cuts and bandages that day! Speaking of the incident, he said, 'He stayed on. He had a concussion and was running around with the bandage on. I normally had a cut, but I never had a cut that day! I remember heading him on the head and he was gone, but fair play to him, he was a giant of a guy. He came back on – just put a bandage on and that was him, no problems. He was a defender, so there were no issues.'

Two more clear-cut chances were created by the Scots in their bid to salvage a draw. Firstly, McCall crossed from the left-hand side and McClair got across his marker to get his head on the ball, but he couldn't generate enough power to trouble an in-form Bodo Illgner. Shortly afterwards, Malpas's cross from a similar position was nodded across goal yet again by

Richard Gough, finding Gallacher free in front of goal. Unfortunately, his header went wide of the target and Germany held on to their clean sheet and, more crucially, the victory that meant Scotland's hopes of progression were over.

The match statistics made for interesting reading as they showed that Scotland had more attempts on goal (17 to Germany's 15) and that Illgner was a busier goalkeeper than Goram, with nine saves to three. Scotland also had more corners (a staggering 14 to two) and won 26 free kicks to the Germans' 13. This emphasised that Scotland were the dominant team, but they lacked that cutting edge and luck where it mattered most, and a side as ruthless as the defending world champions punished them. This is a point emphasised well by skipper Richard Gough, who said, 'We had a lot of chances. I think I should've scored, Slim [McPherson] should've scored, so we had a good few chances against them, especially at set pieces, but they were clinical. We weren't as clinical as the top teams. When you look through the team sheets and the team they had – Klinsmann and Riedle up front – so that was the quality that they had. Just a typical German team.'

Journalist Hugh MacDonald made the point that this is one of the great but forgotten performances by the Scots, given the result. If you only looked at the scoreline and had not watched the game, you'd be forgiven if you assumed it was a comfortable 2-0 victory for the Germans. Whereas, in fact, if you analysed the game forensically, it was anything but comfortable for the world champions that evening. He said, 'In reading Pat Nevin's book, he talks about the reckless nature of Scotland that night and the adventurous buccaneering way we went about it. But, of course, we were just done by quality in the end. The world's great football clichés: "If you're going to go up against the Germans, you better take your chances," because they'll hang in there, and of course they did. It looks a sort of nothing scoreline, nothing to raise your eyebrows, Germany winning by a couple of goals, nothing much to see here and move on. But it completely belittles the reality of that match, and I think it's one of the great forgotten Scottish performances – probably because we got beat.'

When you look at the chances that were created and the nature of the second Germany goal, and assess the history of the Scotland men's national team, you can understand why some Scotland fans have adopted the myth of "Scotland never get the luck". However, Ronnie McDevitt points out that myth isn't quite accurate and highlights the Moller and Hassler efforts in particular that could've made the scoreline a lot worse. He said, 'A completely different performance, with the Scots having a real go to keep themselves in the tournament, not that it was all one-way traffic as you would expect against the World Cup holders. I recall a fairly even game, with Riedle's opener coming around the half-hour mark. When Effenberg's cross struck Malpas and sailed into the net shortly after the restart, there was never going to be any way back. It really was a freak goal and this gave birth to the myth that all of the breaks had gone against us over the 90 minutes and that we had conceded during two breakaways. Scotland continued to attack and a draw would not have been an unfair result, but the Germans twice saw shots rebound from Goram's posts, so if, as the myth suggests, all the luck had fallen to our opponents, we ought to have been looking at a 4-0 defeat.'

Inside the dressing room, the players were disappointed with the knowledge that they were eliminated from the tournament with a game to play, especially after the effort they had put into the game. Stuart McCall summarised the performance by saying, 'Riedle up top, Klinsmann, Hassler and Sammer in midfield, Effenberg – so on paper it was going to be another tough game. We created more chances in that game. It was an end-to-end game. It was brilliant to play in, and Riedle gets the goal. I remember in the dressing room thinking, because normally we'd expect to be defensive, strong, holding on, but we had genuinely good opportunities and put them under pressure, and we were unfortunate not to go in level at half-time. You know the old story at half-time – "make sure we come out the same again" – and they got the luckiest goal two minutes in. Effenberg wide, cross hit Mo and just looped over the Goalie's head, into the far corner. In fairness, they hit the post and they could've got another one, but so could we.'

Naturally, Roxburgh was gracious in defeat, albeit disappointed that this was another tournament where Scotland would be going home before the postcards. The nature of Effenberg's goal was still very much on his mind when I asked for his analysis of the game. He said, 'The second goal is a freak, that's all you can call it. You could have another 100 matches before you see a freak goal like that. Germany knows how to win. Like we had to give credit to Holland, you have to give credit to Germany, who, I think, were outplayed that night then won the game. They had great players – Effenberg, Klinsmann and so on. They knew how to win and they won despite the other team bombarding them.'

Afterwards, Roxburgh sent his players to go and acknowledge the Tartan Army for the wonderful backing they gave them. Even though the game was ebbing away from Scotland, the fans still sang throughout and gave the team great encouragement to keep going, and their appreciation of the teams' efforts were emphasised by applauding them at full time, and they were still there after the players had gotten showered and changed.

What Roxburgh wasn't expecting was a formal request to go and speak to the fans who remained long after the final whistle had blown. Being a man who fully got what supporting Scotland was all about, he walked across the pitch over to where the Tartan Army were congregated and stood on a bench to address them.

Recalling that experience, Roxburgh said, 'The sad thing was the result and it was exacerbated by our fans, the Tartan Army, putting me into tears. I'd told the players to go out and recognise the fans, and I had to go to a press conference. I remember coming into the corridor and one of the players saying, "Boss, you'll have to go speak to the fans," and I went "What?" and he said, "They haven't left, they're waiting for you to speak to them." It was quite nonchalant the way it was said to me, "Go speak to the fans." I challenge any of my national-team colleagues to ever tell me they've been asked to go and speak to the fans right after a match, especially a match they've lost. So I go and walk along this track, and I must be honest to say that "it was emotional" doesn't begin to describe it because, without doubt in my life in football, it was the most emotional thing that I'd been involved in. The idea that you've played out of your skin, you've lost the game, been put out of the finals despite your efforts, and here's this whole packed section of the crowd, and I don't even know what to say. How can you speak to the crowd? I don't even have a megaphone or anything. I stood up on a bench, if I remember rightly, and there's a big wired fence in front of me with our supporters behind it, and the first thing that came to my mind was, "I suppose I'll need to get my P45 on Monday!" A guy in the front row shouts back, "Me too, Andy," because he'd taken time off his work to go out to the games, and everybody burst out laughing at that, and that broke the tension. I can't remember exactly what I said. I just thanked them.'

Roxburgh also revealed to the fans a conversation he had with opposition manager Berti Vogts after the game. Worried about the prospect of the CIS getting through at the Germans' expense, Vogts pleaded with Roxburgh to ensure Scotland won to help Germany progress to the semi-finals. Roxburgh made it clear that they would do everything they could to win their final game, but it would be for our own pride and not as a favour to them.

He said, 'Berti said afterwards, "I need your help. I need you to beat CIS for Germany," and of course

I said to him, "You don't need to worry, Berti. We'll beat them, but we'll beat them for us." There were two reasons for it. One, we need to do that for our fans, but the second reason that we need to do it is because everybody says we've played well here. They've all said we've played really well in two matches. We need to win the last game to justify our involvement in this final tournament. That's what I told the players as well – only by winning that last game. If we lost the last game as well, they would say, "Ach, they've not played that badly, but you really shouldn't have been there." But by winning the last game, people then could argue we were a bit unlucky and that we definitely deserved to be there.'

Jim McInally also got a taster of the worry Vogts had going into the final games, where Germany were due to face up to arch-rivals the Netherlands in Gothenburg at the same time we were back in Norrkoping to face the CIS. In acknowledging that quality defeated effort and endeavour on the day, McInally revealed the incentive they were due to receive if they won the final game. He said, 'The bottom line is, we were just better than them on the day, and it was a bit of class that got them their goal. There's no doubt, from start to finish, we just outplayed them that day. After that game, we were going to play Russia. Berti Vogts had offered us all a bottle of champagne if we got a result against them. Berti was kind of desperate, because it would've been a disaster for them not to get through, and we all got a magnum of champagne.'

As for the fans, they appreciated the effort Scotland put in that day and won admirers from their German counterparts. Whilst the majority of the Tartan Army had a few drinks with their rivals and the locals in Sweden afterwards, the Beerhunter Tartan Army boys Roy Brunton, John Morrison and Steven Gardner had their Interrail train to catch as they continued their European tour. Ironically, their next stop happened to be in Germany!

In recalling the reception they received from the German support and where they went next, Roy said, 'Everybody always remembers, if anything, about Sweden at the Euros, it was after the Germany game where we stayed behind for about three days! Andy Roxburgh got really emotional about that. I remember coming out of that game and the Germans that were left and lined up, and I remember one of them shaking my hand and saying, "Friends of the world." I thought this was brilliant. And they're all applauding us as we had to leave. We had to be in Rostock in East Germany that following morning, that was the problem!'

Whilst the Beerhunter boys were off to Germany before returning to Norrkoping in time for the final match, it was the end of the adventure for groom-to-be Douglas Smith and his best man Eric. Attending two Euro '92 matches against the reigning European and world champions is as good an activity for a stag weekend as you could hope for, as well as having Rod Stewart buy you a round.

Douglas got married a month later. When I asked him if the adventures of Gothenburg and Norrkoping got mentioned in his wedding speech, he replied, 'No, but my best man did! He brought up something about how friendly the young blonde girls were in Sweden, they were very accommodating, and he had an envelope, and in this envelope, there was certain information you could have at a certain price! I wasn't that drunk, was I? He also mentioned how nice it was to be back somewhere where the beers were a bit cheaper rather than what it was costing in Sweden.'

That evening, the other Group B match was played in Gothenburg and was a repeat of the 1988 final between the Netherlands and the Soviet Union, except they were under their new guise of the CIS. The match ended goalless in a largely uneventful game, though Marco van Basten did have a goal controversially disallowed for offside, and left the Group B table in a very exciting position, with Germany and the Netherlands level on three points and the CIS on two from their drawn games, with Scotland sadly on zero points despite their valiant efforts against the European and world champions. The Russians were banking on a victory against a Scotland side with nothing to play for except pride as being enough to overhaul either the Germans or the Dutch.

Oh, how their plans would come crumbling down!

All we are saying is give us a goal

OUT OF the tournament, but the Scotland men's national team were by no means down. They could take pride in the fact they gave the European and world champions a run for their money in those opening matches and gave everything that they got in the process.

This was acknowledged by the fans at the end of the Germany game as many stayed, even after the players had got showered and changed, to applaud their efforts and went one stage further by demanding that Andy Roxburgh come out and speak to them. As a man who fully acknowledged the efforts and sacrifices that the Tartan Army made to follow their team all over the world, Roxburgh had no qualms in obliging.

Although elimination was confirmed after those defeats, there was still one more game for the Scots to play before they returned home – the CIS, formerly the Soviet Union. You may think that, after facing the sides who had won the 1988 European Championship and 1990 World Cup, this would be a walk in the park in comparison. Well, if you did, you'd be very much mistaken!

For this CIS team were no mugs. They had reached the final of this competition four years earlier, and finished above Italy, who placed third at their own World Cup, to qualify for these finals. Crucially, they were undefeated from their two games against Germany and the Netherlands, with two draws, and were within minutes of defeating the Germans, only to be denied by a Thomas Hassler free kick. Against the Dutch, they rode their luck, as a combination of goalkeeper Dmitri Kharine making three excellent saves in the second half and a Marco van Basten goal wrongly disallowed for offside preserved a goalless draw. If anything, they had reason to believe they were now coming into their 'easiest game' of the group, and some of their players had this mindset, but more on that later.

Scotland were going into the game looking for their first goals and points in the campaign, and Roxburgh was determined to end the tournament on a high. This wasn't just for his players, who'd given him everything but a goal so far in the competition, but also for the fans for their tremendous backing and exemplary behaviour throughout their Swedish adventure.

Even after training, Roxburgh had the fans very much at the forefront of his mind and took the unusual step of ordering the driver of the team bus to stop at a nearby campsite for the squad to meet the supporters. It was an unprecedented thing for an international team manager to do at the time, and it's not something that's been replicated since (although someone can feel free to correct me if there are other examples).

It was once again a brilliant piece of PR by Roxburgh to follow up his post-match chat to the fans at Idrottspark stadium, Norrkoping, by randomly going to a campsite with the team to say hello. It's fair to say that a good few of the Tartan Army at that campsite must've wondered if they were still drunk at this time as they saw the team that they were cheering on had voluntarily stopped by for a chat. They responded in tremendous fashion by talking away to the players and staff, then gave them a send-off chant of 'all we are saying is give us a goal' as the squad walked back to the team bus.

When I interviewed Roxburgh for *Famous Tartan Army Magazine*, he admitted that the act was a spur-of-the-moment thing, and how the players were positive when the decision was taken to greet the supporters. He said, 'That was spontaneous. We knew there was a supporters' camp and we said to the guys, "Right, come on lads, before we go back, we'll go and visit our fans." The boys were great. It was, "No problem, let's go!" We just drove the bus right to it. We didn't tell anyone that we were doing it and we just wandered round. We spoke away to the fans, and some of them were taken by surprise. Once the word spread and people gathered, then there's this thing – and I'm smiling at it – they start chanting "all we are saying is give us a goal", and I said, "I think we should join in that!" McCoist made some comment about people being greedy; it was typical of his sense of humour. We got back on the bus and the boys were really quite pleased they'd done that.'

As Roxburgh mentions, that spontaneous act was well received by the players, who by and large embraced the opportunity to speak to some of the Tartan Army, who'd spent a fortune getting to Sweden and when they got there. The fact that Sweden is an expensive nation compared to the UK makes you appreciate their efforts to get there more, and that was not lost on the players. Captain Richard Gough was just as happy to show his appreciation to the fans for the backing they gave the team throughout the competition up until that point. Giving his recollections of the campsite experience, Gough said, 'All I remember was that a lot of the Scots were just camping. We were going along the road, seeing them all in the road. We got off the bus to go and see them. It was typical that it was like they invaded Sweden, and Jonkoping was a nice place to invade. The weather was great, with it being the Swedish summer. It was good. We just wanted to appreciate them, and they all had a good time as well.'

Kevin Gallacher remembers the campsite visit fondly, although there may have been a tinge of embarrassment, given it was made after two defeats. Recalling that day in an interview we conducted for *Famous Tartan Army Magazine*, Gallacher said, 'I remember going to the campsite. We go in and it was almost apologetic to the fans and things, going around talking to them, and they were brilliant. You can't take that away. They're the Tartan Army. Wherever they've gone around the world they've been phenomenal; everywhere you go it's just fantastic. It was great just to go in there, because I don't know if there's been a national team that's done that, going to a campsite to speak to the fans. It was a great day.'

Fellow squad member Jim McInally appreciated the gesture he and his team-mates were asked to make, highlighting the fact that the players were away from their families and closest friends for a lengthy period, therefore speaking to the supporters was a welcome distraction for them. He was also full of praise for the initiative shown by Roxburgh in thinking about the supporters, even in between matches.

When I asked him for his personal recollections of that campsite visit, McInally said, 'It was good for us, because we'd been away for quite a while, being away from home for quite a bit. I always remember Jackie McNamara [senior] and Ralph Callachan were there. Sweden was always such an expensive place to live in, the best thing for people to do was camp in it. Because the team had done quite well in the two games, it wasn't a worry about going into a hostile environment where you could worry about getting abuse and stuff. It was nothing like that. It was just good to go in, and obviously these guys will still be humble, but all these guys were really humble guys in that team; there was no superstars. And it's just a case were of having a right good laugh, getting photos taken, talking to people, giving them your time. It was unique. It was typical Andy Roxburgh – he was always thinking of supporters and it was a nice thing to do.'

The team then left the campsite to continue their preparations for that final game as they aimed to exit the tournament on a high. As they were getting ready for the CIS, another couple of fans were making their way to Sweden in time for the match.

Kevin Barnett had been working for British Midland Airways for a matter of four months when he won airline tickets in a work's Christmas raffle, whilst a friend of his in Ireland, Gavin Edwards, also won a similar prize. The two then came up with a plan of how best to use them. With Kevin's being American Airlines and his friend's for Scandinavian Airlines, things would work out quite well with the Euros in mind. Kevin takes up the story, 'I started working for an airline called British Midland in August 1991, and their head office was in Castle Donnington, down in Derby, so I went down there to work. It was my first proper job. The first Christmas I was there, December '91, they had a Christmas party, and the Christmas parties they had were brilliant there because they held a huge raffle, and whoever organised it got all their contacts from different airlines to give airline tickets as prizes for the raffle. I won two tickets for American Airlines to go anywhere in North America, and a mate of mine from Dublin I was sharing a gaff with at the time won two tickets with Scandinavian Airlines to go anywhere they flew.

'We decided that we would get two trips out of it, so I took him to Boston and New York a few months later, and then we made a plan, because we knew the Euros were on in Sweden, so he says, "We'll try to get to one of the Scotland games in Sweden." As it got closer to the summer of '92, we basically just made sure we had a wee bit of time off whilst the tournament was on, and we just decided that we'll aim for the final game because there's more chance of us getting a ticket for the CIS game as opposed to Germany or Holland.

'It wasn't well planned. We only had about four or five days off around about the final game. We watched the first couple of games and we were like that, "Fuck it, we're still going for the craic anyway." We flew down to Heathrow for buttons. We were in Terminal 3. These Scandinavian Airline tickets happened to be business class as well, so we had to get suited and booted. We hadn't booked a hotel or nothing; we knew there would be a campsite, so we had a tent with us and a sleeping bag. We got on the flight and we flew to Stockholm. Our plan was to fly to Stockholm, get tickets for the England v Sweden game – supporting Sweden, obviously – and there was a late train to get from Stockholm to Norrkoping at like 2am, so that was the plan.'

As Kevin mentions, there was a game that night he wanted to go to in Stockholm, but he couldn't get tickets (more on that later in the chapter). Hosts Sweden were playing England in the final round of Group 1 fixtures, with France and Denmark facing up to each other in Malmo in the other match. With just two points separating the four sides, things were finely poised, with all four still having a chance of reaching the semi-finals.

Choosing who the Tartan Army wanted to win between a welcoming host nation and their arch-rivals wasn't particularly difficult. However, it was looking good for the English when David Platt volleyed them into an early lead with their first goal of the tournament, and they carried that one-goal lead into the second period. Jan Eriksson then headed home an equaliser from a corner, before Graham Taylor did the unthinkable by substituting Gary Lineker for Alan Smith at a time England needed a goal to go through. Not only that but the England captain was two goals away from beating Sir Bobby Charlton's long-standing record as leading scorer for the English, which has since been beaten by Wayne Rooney. It was a baffling move by Taylor. It would turn out to be Lineker's final act as an England player as Sweden produced arguably the goal of the tournament. Tomas Brolin took a pass from Klas Ingesson, played a one-two with Martin Dahlin and beautifully prodded the ball with the outside of his right foot into the top left-hand corner of Chris Woods's goal. It was a goal worthy of winning any game and it meant Sweden went through as group winners, whilst England were heading out of the tournament and going home to headlines like 'Swedes 2 Turnips 1'. Taylor wouldn't be allowed to forget the substitution of Lineker by the unforgiving English media right up until his dying day.

Tomas Brolin, meanwhile, didn't just become a hero in his homeland. That moment of genius forever etched him into the hearts of the Tartan Army, like Diego Maradona in 1986 and Ronaldinho ten years later in 2002. There would later be a party in his honour once Scotland played the CIS, which will be covered later in the chapter.

Commentator Jock Brown was in between games for his BBC Scotland duties and took the opportunity to go along to Stockholm. It's fair to say that this is one of his favourite moments of Euro '92, in addition to Scotland's brave performances, of course. He said, 'The fondness of my memory was really capped off by watching Tomas Brolin score against England. I was in the crowd going, "Oh, ya beauty!" There was a crowd of us, who covered the other games, that night who went to that game. We booked a car and went away to the game, and I always remember thinking Gary Lineker was hooked. He was about to break the record for goals and I just couldn't believe it. Then Brolin scores and that was the last time we ever heard of Brolin, wasn't it? After that he just got fatter and fatter, I think.'

Jock might've been lucky to get briefs for the game, but Kevin Barnett, who with his friend Gavin, from Dublin, had arrived in Sweden courtesy of a work's Christmas raffle win, opted not to take a ticket, such was the price demands of touts outside the ground. After watching the game at a shopping centre bar, they quickly realised that trouble was brewing as a number of England fans started rioting in the streets of the Swedish capital in reaction to their side's early exit.

The shameful act of those England fans made headline news all over the world and painted them in a horrible light. Having worked so hard to rid themselves of a damning reputation from the early to mid-1980s, culminating in a five-year ban for their club sides from European competition following the Heysel disaster, this was a body blow for those campaigners. That reputation was now rekindled, one people to this day still have about England supporters; they are often dismissed as 'typical English hooligans' as a result of what happened in Stockholm and in Malmo during the course of their opening two matches.

For Kevin, he was concerned about his safety and aimed to get to the train station in one piece before boarding the train to Norrkoping. Recalling the trouble avoidance, he said, 'There was kind of an atmosphere about the place because of the amount of England fans and stuff. Being a Scotsman and an Irishman, we were keeping our mouths shut wherever we were going, in case the English weren't too friendly or whatever. It was fine until an hour before the game and we tried to get a ticket off a tout outside the stadium. They were all wanting silly money, the equivalent of £150 to £200, so we were like, "Fuck that, we're on a budget, no chance we could do that."

'We found like a shopping mall quite close to the stadium and we went in. There was a bar. It was full of England fans, but we thought we'll keep our mouths shut and just watch the game in there. We tried not to celebrate when Sweden scored, et cetera, but being absolutely delighted. Then at the final whistle in this pub, about 50 English fans all got up, walked out the pub inside this shopping centre and just started lifting things up, smashing windows in the shopping centre. It was just absolute carnage. They just fucking decided they were rioting. We didn't know what the hell we were doing or where we were going, so we were wandering about trying to avoid trouble basically. It was kicking off everywhere we went. I always remember big groups of England fans, big groups of polis [police] kicking off everywhere. We were pretty much shitting it, trying to avoid trouble.'

Being close to being caught up in that environment must've been scary for Kevin and Gavin as they scrambled away from the chaotic scenes in Stockholm. But if you thought that his ordeal was over by boarding the train to Norrkoping, then think again!

Arriving in Norrkoping in the early hours of 18 June 1992, Scotland fans were coming off the train having lapped up England's exit from Euro '92. Aware of events in Stockholm, the Swedish police were taking no chances and insisted on identity checks for everyone who was on that train. Sounds harmless, but there was just one problem – neither Kevin nor Gavin had their passports!

Having travelled to the Swedish capital the previous day, they left their passports in an airport locker, along with their business-class attire, before beginning their adventures. This error in judgement led to a couple of hours in a jail cell until the matter was cleared up to allow them to resume their adventures. Kevin recalls, 'Eventually, we get to the train station – I can't remember what time it was; I think it was like midnight or one o'clock in the morning – for the train to Norrkoping. We managed to get on the train to Norrkoping. My recollections are that this train took a couple of hours, and as we're arriving in Norrkoping at like three or four in the morning, getting off the train, everybody was met by Swedish polis. They were paranoid, I think, because this train was coming from Stockholm. They thought there were soccer hooligans on this train.

'As soon as we got off, we had to join a queue, and they were checking everyone's IDs and passports to make sure that you were Scotland fans trying to get to the campsite or whatever. Our problem was, when we flew into Stockholm, we knew that we were flying back from Stockholm, and we thought the next couple of days could be carnage – we didn't want to take passports with us and we thought we'll leave them in a locker in the airport, which we'd done. We were suited and booted because we were on this business-class flight. We left the good clothes in the locker as well and had taken the backpack and the tent. When we arrived in Norrkoping, the polis asked us for ID and passport and we had hee-haw!

'They basically bundled us into a polis van, but we were the only ones in it; everybody else must've had their ID with them, and they took us to the local cop shop in Norrkoping. We told them the story. To be honest, we weren't that upset. It was no big deal. They faxed Stockholm Airport and we had the key with the locker number on it. After a couple of hours of us being in a cell, they were very nice to us. There was no hassle. They came back to us and they had a photocopy of the passports from the locker and they took us in a polis motor to the campsite. They were good as gold, dropped us off, we pitched the tent and got a few hours kip, got up, got talking to a few people, managed to suss out a couple of spare tickets for the game that night and then went for a carry-out.'

Kevin's tale could very easily have had a chapter of its own, such was the drama he and his friend Gavin had to endure to get to Norrkoping. Trying to avoid being caught up in the trouble that was unfolding in Stockholm was bad enough, without throwing in a trip to a Swedish jail over an innocuous thing like leaving passports in an airport locker for good measure. It was fair to say that, after this ordeal, they would make sure they enjoyed the rest of their trip from here on in!

Meanwhile, whilst England were making headlines on the front and back pages for the wrong reasons, there was a shock in the other game 320 miles down the road in Malmo. Late entrants Denmark defeated one of the pre-tournament favourites, France, by two goals to one to progress to the semi-finals as runners-up to their Scandinavian rivals. From relaxing on beaches just three weeks earlier to being one game away from the final of the European Championship was remarkable in itself. Surely they couldn't go all the way, could they?

With Group 1 now completed, it was on to the conclusion of Group 2, with three teams fighting it out for the remaining semi-final places. Arch-rivals the Netherlands and Germany went head-to-head in Gothenburg, whilst the CIS knew that victory over Scotland in Norrkoping would give them a great chance of progression to the last four. Victory for either the Netherlands or Germany would see them top the group and claim a semi-final berth at the Ullevi

Stadium against Denmark, whilst defeat for either side would leave them hoping for a favour from the Scots in order to face Sweden in Stockholm. In the event of a draw in Gothenburg, Germany would definitely advance on goal difference, with the CIS then needing to win by just one goal to oust the Dutch.

Going into the game having drawn with the world and European champions respectively in the opening two games, the CIS arrived in Norrkoping very confident that they would do the job. Perhaps too confident, and this vibe was spotted by some of the Scotland players as the two teams arrived at Idrottspark. Stuart McCall was one who noticed, in particular, the antics of his club team-mate and CIS captain Alexei Mikhailitchenko, who made a popping gesture in reference to champagne ready to be corked once they got the job done. McCall said, 'The CIS bus pulled up and Mikhailitchenko was like, "We've got the champagne under the bus," and I was just focussed on the game. I remember Coisty or Jukey or the Goalie saying they'd spoken to Miko and Oleg Kuznetsov, and they had already booked the hotel for the next phase, and Miko said to the Goalie, "We've got all the champagne under the bus, ready to celebrate."'

McCall wasn't the only one of Mikhailitchenko's club team-mates who had noticed his mind-game tactics. Richard Gough recalls a telephone conversation with his rival captain for the night in the days prior to the game, and that some of the champagne was reserved for some of his club team-mates if they helped the CIS get through. Gough was quick to put him in his place and reminded Mikhailitchenko that Scotland were not going to lie down for anyone in their final game of the tournament.

He said, 'I got a phone call from Mikhailitchenko saying, "Hey, De Capitano, you just take it easy tomorrow now," and I says to him, "We're Scotland, by the way; we don't take any games easy. We're just going to go full out." He went, "No, no. I'll make it worth your while. I'll give you a bottle of champagne. We know you boys like a little drink, so we'll give you a box of champagne," and I went, "I think the Germans have already arranged that," because Roxburgh had told us that Berti had promised us a crate of champagne as well.'

Scotland already had enough motivation to win without Mikhailitchenko giving us a further incentive. The Scots had won many admirers for their performances on the pitch and the exemplary behaviour of their supporters off it, so much so that the two police officers who led the team bus to the ground on their motorbikes donned the away shirts of the Scotland team (one had the number 13 of Pat Nevin, the other sporting the number 17 of Derek Whyte). Ultimately, though, the team were still pointless and eliminated from the tournament, and the mission was to have something to show for their efforts and give the fans a reward for their tremendous support.

Andy Roxburgh made two changes to his starting line-up to freshen things up. Tom Boyd was given his first taste of international tournament football by coming in at left-back for Maurice Malpas, whilst Kevin Gallacher was rewarded for his efforts in his two substitute appearances so far by starting alongside Ally McCoist, with Gordon Durie making way.

Scotland team: Goram, Gough, McStay, McCoist (McInally 65), McClair, McPherson, McKimmie, McCall, McAllister, Gallacher (Nevin 79), Boyd

The teams lined up on a soaking-wet evening for the national anthems. A bit of rain wasn't going to dampen the Tartan Army as they belted out 'Scotland the Brave', an anthem that was appropriate to sum up the team's performances so far. They didn't care that the players were already out, they were still going to cheer them on in hope that they would end the tournament on a high. 'All we are saying is give us a goal' was the battle cry – could the team now respond?

Seven minutes in and the wait was finally over – Scotland scored their first goal of the tournament, and the first in their history of the European Championship finals.

Dave McPherson retrieved the ball on the edge of the area after his initial header was cleared only as far as him, and he laid the ball off to Paul McStay. The 'Maestro' then drilled a sweetly struck shot against the left-hand post, which ricocheted off the left arm of goalkeeper Dmitri Kharine and into the net. At last, the Scots had some reward for all their endeavour in the tournament, and the joy and relief could be heard from the few thousand of Scotland fans inside the stadium.

McStay was officially credited with the goal, although there is some dubiety as to whether it should be a Kharine own goal. BBC Scotland match commentator Jock Brown is in no doubt that if a dubious-goals panel were in place in 1992, McStay would have one less than the nine he netted in a Scotland shirt, but also pointed out we deserved that good fortune. He said, 'The goal-analysis people would change that today! We were two up in 16 minutes. That's no bad, even though there's a bit of luck about the first goal. We were entitled to that, I think, were we not?'

As Jock alludes to, things would get better nine minutes later as the Scots doubled their lead. Boyd played the ball to the edge of the box and Ally McCoist neatly flicked it back into the path of Brian McClair, whose shot then took a wicked deflection off CIS defender Kakhaber Tskhadadze and the ball went past the despairing dive of Kharine, into the bottom left-hand corner of the net.

It was a moment of elation and relief for the Manchester United man, who finally had his first goal for his country on his 26th international appearance. A man often ridiculed by some of the Scotland support and who couldn't understand how he was unable to transfer his prolific club form on to the international stage, McClair had reached the point where he didn't care how the goal came; it was all about getting that monkey off his back. Speaking to thesetpieces.com ahead of the delayed Euro 2020 finals, McClair spoke of his relief by saying, 'It wasn't really the goal I'd dreamed of as a kid. That would have been Gordon McQueen's header against England or, even better, Kenny Dalglish's effort against his old pal Ray Clemence, which squeezed in through his legs against the Auld Enemy at Hampden Park. But they all count and to this day I stand by the fact that my shot was destined for the net from the moment it left my foot – the fact it ended up going into the opposite corner from where it was heading is neither here nor there.'

McClair's strike certainly surprised a lot of the Tartan Army, who'd long given up hope that he would break his Scotland duck. The recollections of Roy Brunton of the Beerhunters Tartan Army's are almost JFK-like in that he could say 'I was there when Brian McClair scored for Scotland' to his friends back home. Recalling that game, Roy said, 'I remember the game against the CIS. We were at the World Cup, so we'd seen them beat Sweden, but to see them win at the finals … Admittedly, Brian McClair got a bit lucky. We've seen Brian McClair score for Scotland – top that!'

The Tartan Army were in joyous disbelief at what had unfolded. Having chanted 'all we are saying is give us a goal' during the Germany game and at a campsite when the team paid them a surprise visit, to see two goals in quick succession was mind-blowing to them.

Grant Fisher gave a good summary of how most of the Scotland support in the stadium felt by saying, 'My main memory of the CIS is actually at the game. It was a standing terrace behind the goal, old-fashioned terrace with crush barriers and concrete steps. The one thing I remember most is a father with a small boy near me, maybe seven years old, and Scotland scored early in that game, first ten minutes if I remember correctly. The crowd went mad, our first-ever goal at a Euros! Needless to say, the little kid didn't like it and cried. His dad had just calmed him down – it probably took five to six minutes – and BOOM! – McClair scored, and the whole place went mental again! And off the boy went again.'

The cocky CIS were now completely shell-shocked. The wind had been completely taken out of their sails when that double whammy of bad luck deflected efforts into Kharine's net. Turning up with the attitude that the job was effectively done before they stepped on to the Iddrotspark pitch, now they were in grave danger of going out of the competition. Instead, it was Scotland who were cruising and Andy Goram was largely untroubled in that opening period as the CIS offered nothing to test a Scotland defence well marshalled by the centre-back pairing of Dave McPherson and Richard Gough.

Captain Gough's performances in particular were coming in for high praise, with some believing he was one of the best defenders in Euro '92. McPherson was also having a good tournament, though he revealed in an interview we conducted for Scottish Football Forums Podcast that having Gough alongside him gave him extra confidence to perform well at that level. He said, 'Goughie's a great player and a great leader. I played with Richard for a number of years and a number of games up until then as well, and I knew him really well. We're good friends and we always got on well together. Playing alongside good players like that makes it easier for you.'

At half-time, Scotland's two-goal lead was not just well received amongst the Tartan Army singing in the Norrkoping rain. Approximately 193 miles away in Gothenburg, Berti Vogts's fears over Germany's chances against arch-rivals the Netherlands were being realised as the Dutch cruised to a two-goal lead of their own at half-time, thanks to goals inside the opening quarter of an hour from Frank Rijkaard and Rob Witschge. The fact that a similar fate was happening to the CIS was of relief to the world champions as they remained on course for a semi-final spot – so long as Scotland didn't surrender their advantage!

Into the second half and again Scotland continued to control the game, creating a couple of half-chances to add to their lead. The best of those fell to Ally McCoist, the European Golden Boot winner who'd yet to find the net in the tournament but in truth never had a clear-cut opportunity up until now. His best chance then came when a Stuart McCall shot deflected to him on the far right-hand side of the penalty area. He went to shoot with his stronger right foot, cut back on to his weaker left to fool the defender and his effort went a couple of feet over the bar.

That was as good as it got for McCoist in terms of goalscoring opportunities at Euro '92, though he, like his team-mates, worked ever so hard for the cause and at times had a thankless task as he was well marshalled by some tough defences aware of his prowess. With 25 minutes to go and the CIS now beginning to throw caution to the wind, McCoist was sacrificed for the third consecutive game as he was replaced by Jim McInally, who was on to give added protection in the middle of the park.

The CIS had by this time brought on Igor Korneev, and he had two opportunities to bring his side back into the game and set up a grandstand finish. Firstly, he picked up the ball on the edge of the area and hit a well-struck shot towards the bottom right-hand corner, only for Andy Goram to make an excellent stop low to his right-hand side. It was the mark of what the Goalie was all about, answering the call when required, having been largely untroubled up until then.

A few minutes later, a dangerous counter-attack left Scotland exposed, and suddenly Igor Dobrovolski was one-on-one with Goram. The striker rounded the Goalie, but his effort was well cleared off the line by McInally, before the ball rebounded into Korneev's path with the goal at his mercy – or so he thought. As he pulled the trigger, Goram flung himself to his left and got his left hand to the ball at close range to make a truly stunning save to keep the Scots' two-goal lead intact.

Whilst Goram takes most of the credit for that second save, McInally's part should not be underestimated as Dobrovolski would've scored but for his initial intervention. It was a moment the Dundee United midfielder, who often doubted whether he was good enough to be a Scotland internationalist, was proud of in what he ranks as his proudest moment in football, representing his country in a major international tournament.

Recalling his 25-minute cameo, McInally said, 'That was the pinnacle for me in a Scottish jersey, especially to go there and actually participate. I always remember in the dugout, we were starting to come under a heavy bit of pressure, and I can remember Tommy Craig saying to Andy, 'Put Jimmy on to tighten things up a wee bit,' and Andy, within a minute or two, told me to get ready. It was just fantastic, not just to get on but then to actually participate in the game where I blocked a shot on the goal line when the boy went round Andy Goram, and I got myself back on to the line and Andy Goram then saved the second one. I think if it had went to 2-1, it could've been trouble then, so it was a big moment. And then we go up the park and get the penalty just after it. To go and contribute was like a dream come true for me.'

That was the biggest scare Scotland would get all night, and McInally wouldn't be the only substitute to make a telling contribution to the game. With 11 minutes to go, Pat Nevin was brought on for Kevin Gallacher in hope that his energy would help Scotland run down the clock. Nevin took this literally as he went for a run down the left flank within three minutes of coming on, before coming face to face with Oleg Kuznetsov. With nobody in support and still suffering from a painful leg injury (remember, he didn't know at the time it was a broken fibula), Nevin decided to turn the Rangers defender inside out – so much so that Kuznetsov gave up – before being brought upended by Tskhadadze inside the box for a clear penalty. Gary McAllister took the resultant penalty and calmly placed the ball low into the bottom left-hand corner, sending Kharine the wrong way, to put the icing on the cake of another excellent Scotland performance.

To those watching at home, or even in the stadium, you could be forgiven for assuming that Nevin wanted to do a bit of showboating to help run down the clock. However, he revealed to me when we spoke for this book that he simply couldn't kick the ball far enough to pass it at least 25 yards and had no option but to go for a mazy dribble. He said, 'The impetus was really special by the time we played the CIS, and that was helped by the fact we knew we wanted to give [the fans] something back. But there was an odd moment. The story I remember most was the goal that I was involved in. Of course, I'm running and I can't kick the ball more than 40 yards, so I end up running the length of the pitch, dribbling, then I get brought down for a penalty, and the only reason I dribbled was because I couldn't pass. It was too painful to pass and there was nobody within 40 yards of me, so I had to keep on running.'

Referee Kurt Rothlisberger blew the final whistle, signalling the end for both nations at Euro '92. For the CIS, it was an embarrassing finale to a tournament that promised so much, having drawn with the world and European champions, only to go out on a whimper having been swept aside by a team whom they totally underestimated.

For Scotland, it was the perfect way to bow out of their first-ever European Championship finals. Three goals, a clean sheet and finally getting the luck on their side that went against them in the opening two matches, particularly against Germany. The magnum of champagne from Berti Vogts would now be on its way, with the Germans progressing at the expense of the CIS, despite being easily beaten, 3-1, by the Netherlands, who went through as Group 2 winners.

They would now face rank outsiders Denmark in Gothenburg in the semi-finals, whilst Vogts's side would face hosts Sweden in Stockholm.

The pre-match arrogance of the CIS had now come back to bite them big time as they crumbled to a side with more determination and more composure on the night, and the Scotland players who had club team-mates in the opposition side weren't going to let them forget it. McClair revealed in a column he gave to thesetpieces.com that fellow Manchester United player Andrei Kanchelskis was shocked by the Scots' approach to the match, which in itself summarised how much they underestimated us. McClair said, 'A former room-mate of mine, Andrei Kanchelskis, took exception with me when – despite not being able to progress at Euro '92 after defeats to Holland and Germany in our first two games – we beat his CIS side 3-0 to prevent them going any further. Maybe he was upset at losing out on the huge win bonus his side had allegedly been offered but Andrei couldn't understand that we would be so competitive despite not having anything to play for. Perhaps that goes to show that, despite playing with me at United for a couple of seasons, how little he knew about my competitiveness.'

That assessment of the CIS being shocked at the Scots' approach to the game is backed up by Richard Gough, who had another impressive game in leading his side on the pitch. He and his team-mates could be happy that they'd given the Tartan Army the send-off they deserved for the backing they gave the team, and he didn't hesitate to go over and show his appreciation afterwards. He said, 'When we played in the game, the Russians couldn't believe it, because we had nothing to play for because we were out of the tournament already, yet we were flying into them. They were a good team as well; they had some really good players, including two at Rangers in Mikhailitchenko and Kuznetsov. We played well, and after the game we went to the Scottish fans who'd travelled to thank them, and it was the end of another campaign, but it was a good campaign. It felt as though we hadn't let ourselves down in any way, because we'd played well in the three games.'

Meanwhile, Stuart McCall and his Rangers team-mates were not going to let Mikhailitchenko and Kuznetsov off lightly, in particular captain Mikhailitchenko for his pre-match champagne-popping gestures. He said, 'We go out and we had more good fortune in that one game and wish we had one part of it in the other two games. Paul hits a great shot, but it's an own goal, because it hits the post and goes in off the goalkeeper. Brian McClair gets his first-ever goal for Scotland after 20-odd games, with a big deflection. And then we get a penalty late on. The game couldn't have panned out any better. Not only did we win it, we get three goals and the supporters were brilliant. Unfortunately for my two fellow team-mates, they were a bit sick, and I remember getting back on the bus and looking over saying to Miko, "Can we get your champagne on our bus now?" because we were out to party that night. He was just stony-faced. He was absolutely gutted, because their game plan was not to get beat by Germany, not get beat against Holland, and then walk over Scotland because they're out of it and we were the weakest team in the group and that.'

Continuing his analysis of the tournament, McCall said, 'It was a really good way to finish a tournament which we'd enjoyed, we done well in, we gave everything we had. Coming back, we got received well by Scotland as a whole, because they were quite proud of the efforts we'd done. We didn't get embarrassed, put it that way!'

McClair, McCall and others no doubt enjoyed rubbing the result into their team-mates after the game, whilst for some there were other personal reasons to appreciate the victory. In Kevin Gallacher's case, it completed a form of redemption for being left out of the squad that went to Italia '90, when he believed a place was his, and was reward for not throwing in the towel after that bombshell of being left out.

Now he could cheekily claim that Scotland might've progressed had he started against the Netherlands and Germany instead of coming on as substitute.

In an interview we conducted for *Famous Tartan Army Magazine*, Gallacher summarised the final game by saying, 'We knew it was a nothing game, we knew there would be big changes and we knew we had the opportunity to do it. CIS still had an opportunity. They were a really good side. We just went out and gave it our best shot. This time it went on target and hit the back of the net. It was good to claim that I started the game and we actually won. Maybe if I'd started against Germany, we'd have done something better! Just playing in that game was special. It was a great campaign and I absolutely loved it.'

The players enjoyed rounding off the tournament by comprehensively beating a side who thought they'd won before a ball was kicked. Andy Roxburgh also had good reason to smile and be proud as his players gave the send-off to Euro '92 that he'd wanted, so that they could have something to show for their efforts. That victory certainly gave him that, though he was also cursing the fact that the huge slices of luck they got against the CIS didn't come in the previous matches, which might've made the difference between plaudits and progression to the last four.

Reflecting on ending the campaign on a high, Roxburgh said, 'I think you also help to make your own luck. We deserved to win the game that night and I don't think anybody could argue that we deserved to win the game, and the Soviet Union [CIS] were taken aback. There was a pride in the fact we had finished on a high, but there was still this nagging feeling of "if only". We seem destined to have that printed on our forehead – what if this had happened, that had happened and so on.'

Rounding off their first-ever European Championship finals with a convincing 3-0 win was wonderful for the players' pride and proved that Scotland were no mugs in these championships. But this win was not just for the players to prove something to themselves. As usual with Roxburgh, the fans were very much at the forefront of his mind at the end of the game, and he wasted no time in getting his players across to where the Tartan Army were congregated for one final thank you to those who spent a small fortune in following their team with great dignity in Sweden.

Not only did the players and coaching staff applaud the supporters but they lined up for a team photograph with the fans behind them. This was a statement, showing that the players, staff and Tartan Army were all part of one Scotland men's national team at the European Championship. That photograph is still treasured by Roxburgh to this day in what is arguably his finest hour as Scotland manager. He said, 'I remember saying, "Let's get a picture with the fans." It was a great moment that. We literally went there and had the fans – it was like symbolic – behind us. They were behind us throughout the tournament, and they were behind us in the picture. I've still got that picture here and I think it's an iconic photograph.'

Initially, some of the players were perplexed by the manager's request as it came across as celebrating failure, when the bottom line was Scotland were going home the next day. That was the impression Pat Nevin got when Roxburgh approached him and Gary McAllister as they were walking towards the tunnel, but they appreciated that going to say thank you to the Tartan Army was the right thing to do.

Speaking about that moment, Nevin said, 'Afterwards, Roxy got something fabulously right. We were walking off, and I was walking alongside Gary Mac at the time, saying winning is to be celebrated, losing or going out isn't. So we're walking off gutted because we're out. We won 3-0 but we're out. We've not let ourselves down but we've not succeeded, that's the story. Roxy comes over and says, "Go on over and celebrate with the fans," and we looked at each other and said, "What? What are you talking about? We're out!" But he said, "You need to go celebrate with the fans." And Gary and I were like, "For God's sake." We were not happy about it. We walked down and by the time we got there to the other end, the fans were chanting and singing and we were like, "We got that one wrong, didn't we?" And Roxy was right, because it was another opportunity to say thanks and hope this isn't the last time we can get there again. Sadly, we still never quite got any further than that, but that was the right thing to do, and certainly by the time we got the photographs in front of the fans, the fans behind us – it's one of my favourite photographs from my entire career – and certainly all of that was correct and it felt brilliant. Again, the Tartan Army has evolved and evolved over time, but that was a night. That was definitely one of the great nights where they took a great jump forward and it felt like unity.'

A bunch of people who certainly appreciated the gesture were the Tartan Army. They knew this was the last game they were attending in the tournament, they knew the weather was horrendous, but that didn't dampen their spirits as they inspired their team to victory. Now their backing was being acknowledged, and this is something that they greatly appreciated.

Jim Brown of West of Scotland Tartan Army was one of those in the crowd that night, and he holds that memory of the team coming up to them for a photograph with great pride. He said, 'The victory and goals we all sought came against the CIS, 3-0, and we played them off the park. The support, joy and delight that day was immeasurable – here was Scotland in the finals, playing for fun. Andy Roxburgh brought the team and backroom staff over to the Scotland supporters at the end of the match for what can only be described as one of the best team photos ever. As we walked back into town for a couple of pints before returning to our supporters' bus, the Swedes were lining the streets and hanging from windows applauding the Scots fans – it was reciprocated, with pride.'

After the game, it was all about enjoying what was left of their Swedish adventures before departing over the course of the next few days. It was also a time for reflection on how much they enjoyed Sweden, whether it was for two weeks or two days. For Kevin Barnett and his friend Gavin Edwards, they could really enjoy the remainder of their short stay after the ordeal of trying to avoid trouble caused by English soccer hooligans and being behind bars for forgetting their passports.

Kevin summarised his experience by saying, 'We had an absolute ball of a day, met some cracking guys at the pub, lots of Anglos who'd moved to England but with fierce Scottish roots. My mate from Dublin was welcomed by the Tartan Army. The craic was absolutely brilliant. The game was brilliant, getting the win and we were all buzzing. After the game, we went back to the pub drinking with these guys, and I remember having an absolutely brilliant night.'

It was certainly 24 hours to remember for Scotland fans. From revelling in England's exit at the hands of the hosts the previous evening to capping off their trip with a victory, it doesn't get much better than that for the Tartan Army. Grant Fisher summarised these thoughts well as he said, 'The one memory I really do have is going to the local bar in Granna the night that Sweden knocked out England, with that famous Tomas Brolin goal. "There's only one Tommy Brolin" was sung all night. Needless to say, the local Swedes loved it. We were plied with free beer and pizza the rest of the night after the game. Then we all watched as the news came on and we saw pictures of England fans wrecking Stockholm as their side was eliminated from the tournament. Having to explain to Swedes when they ask, "You are all British; why do they act like that and you don't?" Hard to explain. The following night, we were also eliminated, but in amazing circumstances as we beat the CIS 3-0 in one of the luckiest 3-0 wins I have ever seen! All in all, one of the best 24 hours of my life. Watching England get beat, getting free beer and food in Sweden – which, as you know, isn't cheap – and then watching Scotland get their first-ever win at a Euros – a fantastic 24 hours!'

It wasn't only the fans who were celebrating. Before their departure the next day, some of the Scotland players decided to go and have a few beers with the Tartan Army in Norrkoping to let their hair down after their endeavours over the previous week. Before they knew it, they were joining in an unofficial Tomas Brolin party, in reference to the little Swedish magician sending the English home before the Scots played their last game.

Stuart McCall was one of those who joined in the party atmosphere that involved a few players getting up on stage to sing some songs of their own. He said, 'When we get back to a big arena or something like that in Norrkoping, England got beat the day before so they were home before us, which was the first time ever, because it was a standing joke Scotland are home before the postcards. It was almost like a Tomas Brolin party – everyone was singing Tomas Brolin. They were all doing the conga. There were Scotland fans in there, Sweden fans in there. And they said "we're having a Tomas Brolin party" because he'd obviously scored against England. I remember Coisty going up and singing a Springsteen song. Derek Whyte went up and sang "Leroy Brown". I remember Archie Knox being there, because they used to let coaches go to games, so Archie was there, and there were another couple of coaches through the SFA; I remember having a beer with Archie. We knew we were out of the tournament, but it couldn't have been a better way to finish a tournament – a victory, England getting home before us for once, and we really had a good night that night. We all woke up the next morning with sore heads, I'm sure!'

Whilst some players were at the Brolin party, others went along to a local casino to unwind, which is something that pleased Ally Wilson. Recalling his experiences of the CIS aftermath, he said, 'Best night was after the CIS win. On the way to the bus station after the pub, we met a few Scotland players who had been in a casino. Had a good chat and laugh with Goram, Strachan, McLeish and Duncan Ferguson.'

It was the perfect leaving party for Scotland, but leave they sadly had to, as we just didn't do enough to advance from, arguably, the toughest group stage the men's national team has ever had in a major international tournament. As Scotland departed, Euro '92 continued on to the semi-final stages, and the drama didn't stop there.

Germany spoiled the hosts' dreams of a home victory by defeating them 3-2 in Stockholm to progress to the final, keeping their hopes of a World Cup and European Championship double alive. They were expected to be joined by the reigning European champions, the Netherlands, in a repeat of their Group 2 clash in Gothenburg. However, Denmark didn't read the script as they shocked the holders by advancing to the final with a 5-4 penalty shoot-out win following a 2-2 draw after extra time. Ironically, the two group runners-up were the ones who would contest the final.

World champions Germany against late entrants Denmark in the final of Euro '92. Almost every neutral had this down as a slam-dunk German victory; that Berti Vogts would emulate his European Championship victory as a player 20 years earlier, that plucky Denmark's luck would run out. To most, it was a foregone conclusion.

How wrong those people would turn out to be!

Denmark completed one of the greatest football fairy tales of all time by delivering an incredible 2-0 win over the Germans at the Ullevi Stadium, Gothenburg. From sunbathing on Mediterranean beaches to European champions. Even Walt Disney couldn't script this one! It was a victory that proved anything can happen in football. And how Yugoslavia and their stars, like Darko Pancev and Robert Prosinecki, must've been cursing their luck at the fact the team who took their place ended up winning the tournament they should've been part of but for political turmoil.

The Danes' victory just curses our luck further. With a few breaks, we could've been into the semi-finals, then you just never know what could've happened. As it was, the statistics of the tournament show that Scotland were placed fifth in Euro '92, courtesy of being the only side exiting the competition to have won a game and not have a negative goal difference.

Effectively, this meant that Scotland were the fifth-best team in Europe – that's pretty good going for a nation that was in turmoil after their World Cup performance two years earlier!

Plaudits on the pitch for the players, prizes off it for the Tartan Army. Not a bad Swedish adventure for Scotland and their supporters!

Plaudits on the pitch, prizes off it

THE SCOTLAND men's national team's first-ever European Championship finals was one to remember.

Sure, the history books will tell you that, ultimately, we achieved the same fate as those who qualified for five consecutive World Cup finals, by failing to get out of the group stages. We were also the first side to be eliminated from the competition after just two games, so there is no 'glorious failure' chapter that could be included in this story.

However, when you assess where this squad had come from in the aftermath of Italia '90, to giving both the world and European champions a real scare, without any household names in their squad, it really was quite a journey; one that isn't often glorified in the same way those World Cup journeys were, nor the next European Championship finals four years later.

This was a journey that began with apathy after Italia '90 – a 'lull', as Andy Roxburgh described it – backed up by a low crowd for the opening qualifier against Romania (along with other factors, of course, as described in Chapter One). A journey that took Scotland through a tough qualifying group, against opposition gearing up for better things at the USA '94 World Cup, and boasting one or two top, world-class players amongst them, on their way to making history by qualifying for their first-ever European Championship. A journey that ended with three gutsy performances against three of the best international sides in Europe.

Perhaps if we had one or two world-class players in our side, we could well have reached the semi-finals at the expense of at least one of the Netherlands or Germany. But that would be doing this group a massive disservice, because each and every one of them gave it everything on the pitch and conducted themselves with great dignity off it. Of course, they got up to all sorts of mischief at times and pulled the odd prank on one another, but there was no over-the-top behaviour that landed players in front-page headlines. It should be appreciated that this group was talented, as well, with many players boasting league-title winners' medals from both sides of the border, plus one or two who had the fortune of playing in European finals.

On the pitch, there was no way you could say the players disgraced themselves; there was no Peru, Iran or Costa Rica scenario here. This was the defending European champions, the Netherlands, the reigning World champions, Germany, and the Euro '88 runners-up, the CIS, under a new name following the break-up of the Soviet Union. It's fair to say they gave absolutely everything in those first two games in particular, then got some of the luck in the final game they perhaps didn't get in the first two fixtures, whilst putting in another excellent performance.

Overall, Scotland were ranked fifth in the tournament with their performances, courtesy of being the only one of the sides that didn't reach the semi-finals to win a game and not have a negative goal difference. Effectively, Scotland were the fifth-best side in Europe. That sounds good, doesn't it?

What this tells you is how difficult it was to get to the Euros in the first place, given there were only eight slots available, so for Scotland to get there and then perform admirably really is an achievement we should appreciate more. When you analyse the three games, you could argue it was one of our best performances at a major international tournament.

This view is shared by journalist Hugh MacDonald. He recognised that this Scotland side doesn't get the credit they deserve for their achievement in qualifying for Euro '92, and for the performances they gave in the ultimate group of death. Analysing our performances, Hugh said, 'The underestimated, the undervalued, the under-scrutinised tournament where we had a head coach who was far ahead of his time! We had a series of players who weren't the greatest players in Scottish Football history, but there were some very good players there who performed to a really good level, and we were extraordinarily unlucky not to get to the semi-finals. If we had got to the semi-finals, it's that great Scottish question – "Who knows?"'

BBC Scotland commentator Jock Brown had been to the World Cup finals in Spain, Mexico and Italy respectively in his capacity with Scottish Television, before switching stations after the Italia '90 finals. But he placed Scotland's performance at their first-ever Euros even higher than their subsequent appearances on the world's greatest footballing stage.

Summarising his memories of the tournament, Jock said, 'Euro '92, for me, was my highlight in broadcasting. I was in Spain, Mexico, Italy, America [though not to see Scotland, who didn't qualify] and England. All of these were great experiences, but in terms of pride and performance and what we achieved, I would say Euro '92 was probably number one. It's one of our finest hours and I can't believe it doesn't get the credit it deserves.'

The media were full of praise for the team's character in such a tough group, which made Euro '92 memorable for them. But what about the players? Having played in previous World Cups, you'd be forgiven for thinking that a European Championship where we were knocked out after two games might not rank as highly in their minds. That wasn't the impression I got when I spoke to a few members of the squad lucky enough to be selected for the finals.

Maurice Malpas played in two World Cup finals and had played in a UEFA Cup Final (ironically, the first leg was in Gothenburg) with Dundee United. He also has nothing but fond memories of Sweden, especially the fact Scotland could boast about being the fifth-best team in Europe. He said, 'That's the biggest thing for me, for somebody to say that I would play in a Scotland team that's in the top eight, or finished fifth or whatever. You go into the tournament as one of the best eight teams in Europe, you've got the European champions there, you've got the world champions there, it's probably the highest standard I've played in. For me to be in the squad, it's the first squad to have that achievement, it was a proud moment. It's forgotten about now, because it's been that long ago since it happened.

'I played in three finals, so that was a massive thing for me, and a massive thing for me was to go and play in the European Championship finals, because that had never been done before. I knew I wasn't one of the best players to have played for Scotland, far from it, but I knew we weren't the best squad that had ever been – previous teams were far better. Our squad had a mentality. That squad had something that people never appreciated. We had a bit of grit and determination and a mindset as a team that had a chance, whereas previous squads were never good enough or whatever. That squad was probably the closest I've been to an international team being a club team, because everybody got on so well. You never had any worries about who you sat with; whether it was at a dinner table or in the coffee lounge, an aeroplane, you were very comfortable. A lot of us had played youth-team football together, sort of growing up together, guys like Pat Nevin, Brian McClair, Coisty, big Jukey. We'd all played in the under-18s and under-21s as a group of lads, so it was as close as you could get to a club side in terms of the mentality and the camaraderie.'

Scotland's other regular full-back, Stewart McKimmie, was another who enjoyed the experience of testing himself against three of the best international teams of that era. In an interview we conducted for Scottish Football Forums Podcast, he said, 'In terms of performance, it's probably one of the best performances overall. The three games, I think the team played very well. Holland beat us 1-0, but we made them work to win it. To have players of that calibre – and they had some fantastic names that played in that Dutch side – and Germany weren't quite as good in terms of household names as the Dutch, but of course Germany always have good sides and they've always got fantastic players. It was a great tournament. It was just unfortunate we didn't get through, but I think we acquitted ourselves well and came away with our heads held high, because we really did well and performed well for the country.'

Malpas and McKimmie could be proud of their performances in the competition, as could Hearts centre-half Dave McPherson. 'Big Slim', as he's known to his team-mates, had an excellent tournament alongside captain Richard Gough and played his part in keeping Marco van Basten, Dennis Bergkamp, Jurgen Klinsmann and Karl-Heinz Riedle at arm's length for large spells. His performances played a part in Walter Smith bringing him back to Ibrox for a second spell with boyhood heroes Rangers.

Recalling his thoughts on Euro '92 in an interview we conducted for Scottish Football Forums Podcast, McPherson said, 'I think it's one of the highlights. The World Cup, because that's the pinnacle of world football, is always going to be up there, but Euro

'92 it tends to be forgotten, but for me it should be highlighted, because it's two groups of four, and it was almost like a group of death we were in. Holland, Germany, the CIS, and we definitely managed to hold our own. Holland, lost a goal through Bergkamp. Germany are an unbelievable side, and we had chances against them that we should maybe have got something out the game, and then winning the last game. I think Euro '92 tends to get put in the shadows a little bit because it's not the World Cup.'

McPherson also added some compliments about the approach Scotland took in the finals, where they weren't content to sit in against their elite opponents; they wanted to take the game to them. It's not something you would imagine from a side of our calibre now, as he explains, 'That was the good thing about the tournament – we tried to play attacking, creative football and we created chances because of that, instead of ten men behind the ball. Can you imagine if Scotland qualified now and we were in a group of Holland, Germany and Russia? It would be eye-watering!'

McPherson's central-defensive partner also had a campaign to remember. Richard Gough was colossal throughout the tournament as captain of the team, with his performances leading to many observers saying that he was worthy of being named in a team of the tournament, though UEFA's official verdict picked Germany's Jurgen Kohler and France's Laurent Blanc as the centre-back pairing in their best XI. Not that it detracted from Gough, who admitted that the three games rank very highly in terms of his own performance levels for his country, and more importantly that the team could not have given any more in their attempts to topple three of the best international sides in Europe.

Assessing Euro '92 and what it meant to the man who was captaining Scotland in the land of his birth, Gough said, 'It was one of the better Scottish teams during the piece, and it will always be up there in my mind. For the way the team played, on a personal level I played consistently, three really good games for Scotland in as high a level as I've played, and the team performed as well as we could when you think that the two favourites went through to the semi-final. Playing against the two best teams, we didn't let ourselves down in any way, and the fans and press showed that as well. They knew we couldn't have done any more, we couldn't have performed any better than we did. There's been a lot of tournaments where we haven't performed as we should've. This was a tournament that we did – and we still didn't get through!'

Another flame-haired Rangers player who could be proud of his performances in the tournament was

Stuart McCall. The midfielder put his body and soul into the cause as he came up against the likes of Frank Rijkaard, Matthias Sammer and club team-mate Alexei Mikhailitchenko. McCall also emphasised the team spirit in the camp by being able to not only dish out the odd prank and joke, as he emphasised by planting traps in Ally McCoist's room, but also taking being on the receiving end with good grace – a case in point: his being flung in a water fountain on his birthday.

Having impressed at Italia '90 after a late introduction to international football, McCall continued to impress not only the management team but also the Tartan Army, who took him to their hearts. Despite being born in Leeds and having a broad Yorkshire accent, he was recognised as one of our own, given his parents came from Scotland, and his performances showed that he was proud to represent his real country!

Euro '92 was a tournament McCall could look back on with pride, especially with the fact we ended on a high, and he summarised the experience by saying, 'It was the first time that we'd got to the Euros, so that was a massive achievement. My overall feelings of the tournament are the Swedish people were absolutely fantastic, and if you boil it down, there were only eight teams there; the likes of Spain, Italy, Portugal, the big nations who've won tournaments, weren't there and we were. We come back with, I say, a decent reputation. We were up against Holland and Germany, two top-class sides, and the CIS just thought they had to turn up to beat us and that was it, so it was nice to get a victory!'

Of course, for regulars in the starting line-up like Gough, Malpas, McPherson, McKimmie and McCall, it's perhaps easy for them to recall fond memories of Scotland's first-ever European Championship finals as they played in the majority of the games. Only Malpas from that batch didn't play in all three matches as he was rested for the finale against the CIS. But what of those who weren't in the starting line-up and had to be content with a place on the bench, hoping that their moment would come?

For midfielder Jim McInally, we've established that he considered his cameo role in the final game the pinnacle of his career, being able to play some part for his country at a major international tournament. Having been part of Andy Roxburgh's youth sides that won the Under-18 European Championship a decade earlier, being able to represent Scotland in the senior version of the competition was a thrill for the Dundee United man.

McInally said, 'I came from Castlemilk in Glasgow, dreaming about all my career when I was a wee boy, dreaming about playing football at a higher level, playing for Celtic, playing in cup finals, playing for your country and then actually representing your country at a major tournament. I always remember my first season at Dundee United when we got to the UEFA Cup Final. I remember thinking, "I can't top this now. Where do you go from here? This is my first season and we've just played Barcelona. Playing in a cup final, getting my first cap for Scotland that year." Then along comes '92, when I'd had a blighted season with injury and I couldn't see myself making that squad, so to actually make the squad and contribute to the squad it was just brilliant, I'm just so happy that I was able to participate. It's amazing how many people – because of the Euros this year and because of the hysteria that was whipped up in Scotland – spoke to me about the Euros. They ask questions that people have probably never asked about them before. People were wanting to know, "Oh, you played in the Euros. What was it like?" So it's one of those things that everything gets better as you go on. It was just fantastic and I think being in such a nice country like Sweden topped it off as well, because there were so many Scottish fans there. You talk about guys in an international team that don't get on, but we had a great spirit in that team. We had good fun. We trained hard and we played well.'

Not everybody within the squad was content at being the best of the sides who didn't progress at Euro '92. Winger Pat Nevin believed that anything was possible, as proven by the fact that the tournament's late entry and rank outsiders, Denmark, went all the way to become European champions. Whilst there was an acknowledgement of how well Scotland performed, Nevin also got a sense of what might've been had we got past either the Dutch or the Germans.

He said, 'You needed good enough players, you needed the group together, you needed a good technical side of the game. You needed it all to be able to be ultra-competitive against the world champions, the European champions and against Russia – and we were! There was no embarrassment about going out, but we were so disappointed. See, when you look at it and you look at who won it, you think, "Us against Denmark? I'd be happy to take that one," and I think we could've done them. They had some great players, but they were, by some distance, the team we thought were weakest in the whole event, yet, somehow, they managed to get through and won. So you need everything. One of the things you need is luck, and we didn't get it.'

The players had good reason to be proud of the way they conducted themselves on and off the pitch. They earned lots of plaudits, both from the media back home and even abroad, for their efforts throughout the competition. But it wasn't just the players who were getting praised for their conduct at Euro '92.

Scotland's adoring fans, the Tartan Army, won many admirers for their behaviour in Sweden that saw them mix well with the locals and rival supporters, as well as a self-policing approach to ensure any little incidents of misbehaviour were nipped in the bud. Their reputation didn't go unnoticed by UEFA, who named them as best supporters at the finals.

It was an incredible compliment to the Scotland fans for the way they conducted themselves during the couple of weeks they were in Sweden. When you contrast that with the behaviour of some of their English counterparts, who were rioting and tarnishing their reputation so much that there was a threat from European football's governing body over hosting the next finals four years later, they shone like a beacon in comparison. Instead of fighting with the Swedish police, there's a famous image of one fan receiving a kiss on the cheek from a local policewoman at the Ullevi Stadium, Gothenburg, proving that our presence was welcome.

According to Ronnie McDevitt, this act of love, so to speak, was what tipped the balance in the Tartan Army's favour when UEFA made their decision on who was receiving the best-supporters accolade. He said, 'In my view, the fans-behaviour award was literally sealed with a kiss. Had it not been for the photographer capturing the image of the fan with the policewoman and its worldwide distribution, personally I think the prospects of the award from UEFA would have been greatly diminished.'

Whether it was sealed with a kiss or not, nobody could take away the achievement from the Tartan Army, and it's something they can look back on with immense pride. Euro '92 may have been the tournament where the good reputation of Scotland fans took off and carried on since, as backed up with a similar award from FIFA after the France '98 World Cup, but the foundations of the Tartan Army as we know them had been laid some time before. According to Hugh MacDonald, the Spain '82 World Cup was the launch pad for the reputation of Scotland fans being viewed in a more positive light as they adopted the attitude of having a good time regardless of the result.

Hugh takes up the story, 'There was a sea change in the Tartan Army. I think the early days of it, personally, were a round about the early 1980s. The Tartan Army in Spain. I didn't go, but a mate of mine, Iain Scott, who's sadly no longer with us, he went and he noticed that everybody was there for a jolly, everybody was relaxed – maybe it was the Spanish sunshine, the sangria and that – and there was no aggression. I always think it was a reaction to England as well – England hooliganism and England fighting – and I think there was an element who thought, "We're not like them. We're going to be the exact opposite. We're going to kiss policewomen or leave huge tips in the bar, clean up," and it has continued.

'It was almost a conscious thing – "We're not going to be like England. We're going to be the team that people like to see arrive on their doorstep. We're going to be boisterous, probably going to have too much to drink, but we're not going to have riot police chuntering after us." And I think the real epitome of that was Sweden. Scotty always said, "There were real signs of it in Spain," but I think, ten years later, it really was a thing now. The Tartan Army had decided, in some kind of unofficial, informal and unwitting vote, that they were going to be the good guys, they were going to be there for enjoyment's sake, and the Fair Play award franked that. Once that had happened, it was almost set in stone, wasn't it? The die was cast and it's been great ever since.'

Getting UEFA recognition certainly was a massive compliment to a group of fans who were keen to follow their country into uncharted territory, being the first Scotland men's national team to participate at the European Championship finals. No matter what means they took, whether it was plane, train or bus, it was all worth the effort when they received this award.

Jim Brown from West of Scotland Tartan Army, who'd organised a bus trip to Sweden, summarised the whole thing very well by saying, 'Scotland and its supporters had worked hard to establish a reputation as fair-minded, committed and friendly football supporters. I and all of my friends and fellow supporters did not need to be told to behave; it was second nature. We done everything we could to enhance this, from putting a sign on the front window of the bus in five languages saying "Scottish football fans on board" to cover each country we were travelling through – it seemed to be well received – to transporting a message and gift from the Lord Provost of Glasgow to the mayor of Jonkoping. I met the mayor with Tommy Madden, who worked at Glasgow City Council, in his office, who, in addition to a cup of tea, insisted that we sampled (very large and many samples) of the local hooch. A photo appeared in the local paper and the city residents thought this was great. When the fans were awarded the Fair Play award, I had a feeling of immense pride. That is what football is all about – be committed, be passionate, be noisy, but above all ensure that you and everyone else enjoys it.'

Like Jim, every one of the fans I was fortunate to speak with, whether on a Zoom call or by electronic communication, has nothing but fond memories of Euro '92. Each and every one of them had some great tales – some were too explicit for this book and some are likely holding on to more amazing stories by adopting the 'what goes on tour, stays on tour' mentality.

The Beerhunters Tartan Army boys Roy Brunton, John Morrison and Steven Gardner shared many good stories from using their Interrail tickets to get them across mainland Europe during that summer. They were also conscious of the impression they and the rest of the Tartan Army were having on the locals, including the authorities, who were far less concerned about potential trouble as they were for after England matches. Roy said, 'There was a lot of police on duty, especially on Norrkoping High Street, but as we were walking by them, they were clapping us. You know the Swedes, they're big laddies, but they knew there wasn't going to be any trouble.' John then jokingly suggested a reason why they, in particular, were popular, by adding, 'I think it was the karaoke machine, to be honest. It filtered through Europe fast.'

Steven reminds us that the Euro '92 was about much more than following Scotland at a major international tournament. This was also about enjoying a holiday with friends and meeting new people along the way. He said, 'It was the first lads' holiday, as well as going to the Euros. We hadn't had an awful lot of pressures. We'd saved the money to go. We could go, enjoy ourselves and have a great time, and it was an adventure. The football was great, meeting all these people was great and having beer and experiences was great. It was an adventure and it was fantastic.'

John echoes those sentiments, as well as appreciating the fact he got to experience different cultures by taking the trip to Scandinavia. By choosing to go down the Interrail route, there was an added excitement for him, Steven and Roy as they had freedom to go wherever they wanted within most of mainland Europe, and they made the most of that privilege.

Recalling the adventure, John said, 'I would say getting to see new cultures, especially Scandinavia for the first time, and realising that Scottish people are loved around Europe and the world. I remember everyone just loving us, whether that was the booze or the situation, and also to see Scotland win 3-0 at a major championship was brilliant at the time. We went on the back of a whim. Each night, we didn't know where we were going to end up travelling to, and that was a nice excitement as well. I love travelling and that was one of the best travelling experiences.'

Roy summarised his feelings on the trip by ranking it at the very top, but he also made a very good point that sums up how much the world has changed since 1992. The internet wasn't even a thing back in the early 90s, let alone social media and camera phones; this was an era in which you had to wait until you got home to see what pictures were taken after they were developed, as opposed to instantly in the present day. Roy said, 'It's the best Scotland trip that I've ever been on. There was just something special about it. They were better days because there was no "Oh, there's John fallen through a plate-glass window – snap," then two minutes later it's on Facebook. You didn't know what photos you'd taken until you got them developed when you got back.'

The story of Euro '92 was where the friendship of the three Beerhunter Tartan Army lads began, and it's a testament to them that they remain in touch to this day. For others, they drifted apart from those they took the trip with; not necessarily through fall outs, but such is life that these friendships can drift apart. Kevin Donnelly, author of a Tartan Army tales book called *Chancers, Dancers and Romancers* and regular follower of the Scotland team home and abroad, ranks Euro '92 as one of his favourite experiences, even though he doesn't keep in touch with the group of friends he went with. He also gave special praise for the team's efforts in Sweden, which wasn't always the case for Scotland sides at a major finals as, in his opinion, there were times where some teams and individuals didn't give it all for the cause. When you compare and contrast previous tournaments, he may have a case, although that's a discussion for another book.

Reflecting on these championships, Kevin said, 'When I look back at Euro '92, I went with two other guys that I'm not in contact with anymore for a variety of reasons, mainly just drifting apart. At that time, you had a good team, which had a good manager, that somehow qualified out of nowhere for a tournament, and any chance to visit Sweden should not be ignored. Ultimately, they maintained the record of not being good enough to qualify out of the group. It was a very hard group. But I think they gave their absolute best in every game. I don't think you could say that about Italia '90. Maybe that led them to try as hard as they did. Maybe they still had the hangover from the Costa Rica game or the Brazil game that slipped away, I don't know. But, to me, they gave it a good go and I don't think you can ask any more than that of any Scotland team.'

You really couldn't argue with Kevin's thoughts on the team's performances at their first European Championship. They really did give their all in the three matches against incredibly tough opposition. Nobody could be accused of being half-hearted in their approach and they left everything on the pitch.

The same could also be said of the Tartan Army for the backing they gave their team and their behaviour during the competition. They were well looked after in Sweden, who were excellent hosts, and it wasn't just the locals who looked after them.

Marjorie Nimmo ran the Scotland Travel Club, now known as the Scotland Supporters Club (SSC), in the early 90s and could offer a more personal service to the several hundred members, compared to the near 20,000 in the SSC at the time of writing. There were times she went above and beyond the call of duty, like when Jim Brown's wife, Lillian, and 15-month-old daughter, Lynsey, joined him in Sweden. Jim takes up the story of when Marjorie offered to take care of Lynsey during the final game against the CIS, whilst summarising what the tournament means to him as a whole, 'It was a pleasure to have attended Euro '92. The team gave what they had to give, as did the supporters. I, however, have a couple of special memories. My wife, Lillian, had given birth to my eldest daughter, Lynsey, a few days before the Bulgaria qualification match at home. Little did I know that, around 15 months later, mother and daughter would join me in Sweden at the finals. A coach trip to Sweden would have been too much, so I arranged to fly them to Gothenburg and I met up with them there for the game. They then stayed at my hotel for the duration, before they flew back. They attended all the games with me ... making hundreds of new aunties and uncles, Scots and Swedes alike. At the match against the CIS, Marjorie Nimmo of the Scotland Travel Club saw me with Lynsey on my shoulders just after half-time. She came over and insisted on taking Lynsey in her buggie for a short time. She brought her back 40 minutes later. She had been pushing her around under the stand and at the front of the terrace. A wonderful woman!'

Most fans departed Sweden after that final game with the foresight that it was unlikely that Scotland were going to advance from the group of death. One fan who pre-planned an extended stay in hope of Scotland progressing into the semi-finals was Ronnie McDevitt. Although he didn't get the dream scenario of Scotland being in the last four, he was fortunate enough to get a ticket for the match between the Netherlands and Denmark in Gothenburg. With the Danes progressing on penalties, maybe it was the next-best thing in that he saw an underdog advancing to the final – and eventually winning the tournament! He gives a detailed summary of how much Euro '92 meant to him, even if there is a tinge of regret in not taking up the offer to go and see U2 during his trip.

Ronnie said, 'Along with my month-long excursion to the 1990 World Cup, Sweden was the longest trip

I ever enjoyed. Personally, I would say Sweden is probably not in my top ten, but certainly makes the top 20 of trips, but it is difficult to compare a five-day holiday with a four-week jaunt. After both of those month-long adventures, having enjoyed close to 30-odd successive nights out, I was left with a feeling of emptiness for a while at getting back to the all-work-and-no-play routine. I experienced a real sense of anti-climax when it was all over and used to fantasise about not having to work and going on holiday all the time. It was, of course, good to have attended the Euros at last and the final was a memorable occasion, but the semi between Holland and Denmark, which I also attended – with the Danes winning on penalties after a 2-2 draw – was actually a better game. Regrets? Well, I guess it would have been nice to have seen U2 live …'

The impact the Tartan Army had in Sweden was not at all lost on the Scotland squad or the management team of Andy Roxburgh and Craig Brown, having taken the time to go and applaud the supporters, have a thank-you photograph after the final game and even stopping by at a local campsite just to go and have a chat with them. All of this is just an inkling of what the Scotland supporters meant to them.

Brown would eventually succeed Roxburgh nearly 16-months later and replicate his success by guiding

Scotland to consecutive tournaments, this time in reverse, with the European Championship in 1996 being followed by the France '98 World Cup. Being Roxburgh's right-hand man at Euro '92 means just as much to him as leading his country at those respective finals, and he gave his summary in an interview we conducted for *Famous Tartan Army Magazine*. He said, 'I remember the atmosphere in Sweden was good. I remember we took the team bus to the fans. A lot of the fans were staying in tents outside Gothenburg. It was a very popular visit when the team bus went in there, and they all came out of their tents to meet the players. That was an unusual environment in which to find the Tartan Army. They're very resourceful the Tartan Army guys, as you know, but the support was terrific in Sweden. The objective is to make the fans happy, and they deserve to be made happy because of the expense they go to, the resources they have to find to get to the European Championship, even just to get to away games. The respect Andy and I had for the fans is quite incredible. So to give them a good victory after a couple of disappointments – and I don't think the performances were too bad; we were playing a couple of good teams – to compete with them as well as we did was worthy of credit.'

The praise for players and fans is there for all to see, and there's no question that they deserve full credit for the way they represented their country, whether it was on the park as a player or off the park as an unofficial ambassador for their country. And the behaviour of both the players and fans away from the stadiums is there for all to see, so much so that there was no front-page scandal involving them that had occasionally been the case in previous tournaments.

We should conclude this story of Scotland's Swedish adventure by covering the man who made it all possible – Scotland manager Andy Roxburgh.

A man whose appointment was ridiculed back in 1986 when he succeeded Alex Ferguson, Roxburgh overcame some difficult obstacles to accomplish something that none of his predecessors were able to achieve by taking Scotland to a first-ever European Championship. In addition, he was the first of two men to take Scotland to two consecutive international tournaments.

It's an incredible accomplishment for a man who worked his way up the ranks within the Scottish Football Association from his job as director of coaching, predominantly working with the underage sides, with some success. People who ridicule the appointment forget that Roxburgh himself was just as surprised as they were when the late Ernie Walker, the SFA secretary, asked him to become Scotland manager. Roxburgh revealed to me that on only one occasion, before he was asked by Walker, did the idea of him becoming a future manager of the men's national team enter his head, as had been suggested by the late Jock Stein just months before his untimely death whilst managing his country in a World Cup qualifier in Cardiff.

Reflecting on his appointment, Roxburgh said, 'When Ernie Walker came to me on a Wednesday morning at 11 o'clock, he said, "The International Committee would like you to be the manager of Scotland." I'll be honest, I never actually thought about that idea. Although I managed the underaged teams, that idea was beyond me, because I wasn't a club manager. I said to him, "I'll need to have a think about this," and he went, "Aye, that's fine. The press conference is at half past two in the afternoon." So it was like, "You don't have a choice here!" I remember saying, "OK, I'll do it, as long as I keep my current job," and he went, "Aye, that's fine, no problem, on you go." That's what triggered it, and the only time I can honestly say that this idea that I would have anything to do with the national team in a way was Jock Stein.

'I sat in the back of a car with him going to a conference in Florence. We'd been to see Graeme Souness play for Sampdoria, and we were on our way there and Jock turned to me and he said, "Have you ever thought about doing my job?" I laughed at him and said, "You're kidding me on," and he said, "You must be ambitious?" I said, "I'm ambitious for Scottish football," and he said, "That maybe also means doing my job." I then said, "Come on, there's no way I can ever be involved with your job," and he just turned to me and said, "Well, maybe you should think about it." I remember that always stuck in my mind, thinking, "Why on earth would he say that to me?" This was, I think, in the June, if I remember rightly, before he died, only months before he passed away. That was the only time that thought had been planted in my head. Then the second time was Ernie Walker walking up to me and saying, "By the way, you've got until this afternoon to decide."'

Overcoming the negative press reaction to his appointment was hard enough. Roxburgh then had to endure a tough Euro '88 campaign, where we finished a distant fourth in the group. Things started coming to fruition by reaching the 1990 World Cup finals, although the performance against Costa Rica almost brought things back to square one, reflected, of course, in the attendance for the opening qualifier against Romania. In a campaign decimated by injuries, Roxburgh was still able to lead his team into uncharted territory, which is a testament to his character. Taking Scotland to Euro '92, and performing so admirably in the tournament against such heavyweight opponents, is arguably his finest hour.

Journalist Hugh MacDonald has nothing but admiration for Roxburgh and the journey that led to him becoming Scotland manager, which started all the way back to his teaching days. MacDonald said, 'I was so pleased for him, even on a personal level. I actually knew Andy as manager of Carolside Primary School, because, when I was a kid, I was at St Joseph's, Busby, and Andy was a teacher at Carolside, and he was coaching the primary school side. I always thought, the way he's risen in the world, I was pleased for that meritocracy, that a guy had got the job, not because he was the best centre-half or had been a great goalscorer but because he'd been looked upon as an innovative coach. He had success with Scotland at an underage level, unprecedented success, and I remember talking to guys like Walter Smith about him. He was well regarded by Walter and people like that, who came from a different footballing background, so I was pleased for him. I was genuinely pleased for Scotland as well, but again it's a great thing looking back. One of the feelings was it was crushingly disappointing to go out. That never leaves you. There was a lot of what ifs – the Germany game, in particular. There was a lot of feeling of disappointment that, yet again, we'd gone out in the group stages.'

Of course, no team can function without the support of the players, and Andy Roxburgh had most of the players' backs throughout that campaign. Yes, there were fall outs with individuals along the way, as emphasised by Steve Nicol's decision to retire from international football mid-qualifying campaign, but those were few and far between as the majority of the players formed a good relationship with Roxburgh and his assistant, Craig Brown.

It probably helped that a number of players from Roxburgh's Scotland youth sides of the early 1980s were part of the class of '92, including Jim McInally. The Dundee United midfielder often questioned whether he was worthy of being part of the senior Scotland set-up, and it's a testament to Roxburgh's man-management skills that he helped McInally believe that he was just as deserving to be part of his plans as anyone else in the squad. Nullifying the threat of Bulgarian talisman Hristo Stoichkov in a hostile atmosphere in Sofia went some way to McInally proving that he was worthy of an inclusion in the 20-man squad that went to Sweden.

When I asked for his thoughts on Roxburgh, McInally said, 'First and foremost, I can go back to our youth team and we were the only Scottish youth team to win a European tournament, and then we went to the World Cup in Mexico the next year and got to the quarter-finals. So I go back then to Andy – I had a good rapport with him. If you go back to our Euro '92 team, there was quite a few of us played in those teams. Myself, Pat Nevin, Brian McClair, Paul McStay, Dave McPherson, so I think there was a bit of loyalty there, where Andy was always comfortable with us, certainly with me. Some guys were first choices anyway. There was a loyalty there with Andy, but there was always a shrewdness about him as a manager, as a tactician. Every time you played an international football game, you knew everything that the opposition were going to do, you countered it and you played against it, and he was excellent at that.

'I knew he came through a tough time, but I think '92 would be the pinnacle of his time as a manager, I would imagine. I also think he never got the respect he deserved from some senior players, and I'm not talking about senior players who eventually played for him. I'm talking about players who, when he started, there were some players who should've been playing for Scotland that turned their back on Scotland because they didn't quite fancy Andy as a manager, and I felt sorry for him then, because he was a wee bit more modern in his ideas, in the way he wanted to do stuff, and I think some of the older pros didn't see that as the way ahead. They just saw someone more like a school-teacher type, and Andy was more than that.

He didn't get an easy start; he had to go and prove himself, and I think he done it really well.'

This was as good as it got for Roxburgh. He stayed on for another 14 months and oversaw a difficult USA '94 World Cup qualifying campaign that included Italy, Switzerland and Portugal. An opening 3-1 defeat away to the Swiss, when Richard Gough was sent off for inexplicably catching the ball after it bounced off a water sprinkler, set the tone for a miserable campaign that saw an end to the World Cup run after five consecutive appearances. The match that best summed up the campaign was a humiliating 5-0 loss in Portugal that saw Ally McCoist break his leg and a famous fallout between Roxburgh and Gough, who never played for Scotland again. This was a sad tale after a famous photograph of manager and captain, side by side, in front of the fans just ten months earlier; a symbol of unity in Norrkoping that had now ended bitterly in Lisbon. After a 1-1 draw with the Swiss at Pittodrie officially ended our hopes of reaching the finals, Roxburgh left his position with two qualifiers remaining, after seven years in charge.

Despite the breakdown of his professional relationship with Roxburgh, that post-match picture still means a lot to Gough 30 years on, so much so that he still has a copy of it in his home in San Diego, where he resides at the time of writing. When I asked him for his assessment of the Tartan Army backing in Sweden and the photographs being published around the world after victory in the final game against the CIS, Gough said, 'The Scottish supporters are pretty fair in a way that, if you give it your best shot, then they'll be happy with you, and they were happy. They stayed after every game. Even when you mention that picture of Andy Roxburgh and myself – I've got that same picture downstairs in my basement and there's a huge crowd behind us. That was a well-remembered picture. It's one of the few pictures I've got downstairs. I've got a picture of Van Basten and myself with Rijkaard, so those were the games that you remember. It was a good tournament for us and for the supporters as well, UEFA giving them supporters of the tournament as well, so it was good.'

One wonders if Andy Roxburgh would've been better off ending on a high with that performance at Euro '92. However, he felt a duty to carry on and start a rebuilding process for future tournaments, and this was an era before life-changing salaries, where a manager can afford to take a year or two out of the game in between jobs, which wasn't the case in 1992. We don't know for sure if he had any other job offers on the table in the aftermath of Euro '92, not ones better than the Scotland men's national team manager, anyway, but circumstances did change when he handed in his resignation once our World Cup fate had ended. His right-hand man and successor, Craig Brown, revealed in his autobiography, *The Game of my Life,* written in 2001, that the SFA tried to persuade Roxburgh to stay, but the effects of the Portugal game sealed his fate and that he now had tempting offers on the table, one of which he accepted as he became UEFA's technical director. Brown said, 'The SFA International Committee did discuss it with him with a view to changing his mind, but he explained that he felt his team had died during that game against Portugal. He had made up his mind and that was that. I believe, though I do not know for certain, that Andy had many offers on the table – and indeed he has since become UEFA's Director of Football Development, a very responsible job and one that I know he enjoys immensely. As technical director of UEFA, he is responsible for 51 countries, and I have attended many of the courses he organises and presents for coaches. All the top coaches attend, and Andy Roxburgh is well respected by all of them.'

At the time of writing, Roxburgh was working in a similar capacity with the Asian Football Confederation and still lives in Switzerland, having moved there when he joined UEFA. It shows how well respected he is that two of the world's biggest footballing governing bodies headhunted him to help head up the coaching network of their organisations. This after becoming the first Scotland manager to lead his nation to a European Championship and consecutive international tournaments. Not bad for a man who was appointed Scotland manager in a blaze of controversy.

So that was the story of Scotland's inaugural appearance at a European Championship finals. It is fair to say that the achievement of getting to the finals was not appreciated as much at the time, particularly as it was viewed as an expectation for a nation who'd reached five consecutive World Cup finals. It is only now, 30 years on and after witnessing a 23-year gap between appearances at major international tournaments, that we can fully appreciate the achievement of Scotland reaching a finals, particularly one with just eight teams in it. To say that we were one of the eight best teams in Europe is something that doesn't get spoken about much, let alone finishing fifth in the competition. How we would bite someone's hand off for that now! The players, fans and management team can all be proud of their efforts that make up this story.

The final words should be left, fittingly, to Andy Roxburgh, the man who guided Scotland to the Euro '92 finals. During his seven years in charge, Roxburgh always had the fans at the forefront of his mind, mainly because he recognised that he and the players were fans themselves and were representing them in the finals. He summed up these emotions perfectly with this statement:

'We've always had this empathy, because, basically, you are fans. I'm often asked about, "Why did you wear a tartan scarf when you played Sweden in the World Cup?" – and I've always told everyone that it was symbolic, because, at the time, it was my way without words of letting the fans know that we were also fans, and if they were hurting then we were hurting. Of course, when you are professionals, you're not fans on the park, but you're playing for the fans. You've got to be professional; you've got to take that excess of emotion out of it, but in our heart, we were all the same. We started as fans, and once we're finished with it, we'll become fans again. That's exactly what happened with all of us.'

Acknowledgements

FIRSTLY, I would like to thank all of the individuals I have had the pleasure to interview for the book for sharing their respective experiences of Euro '92. From the seven players who played in the tournament, through the management team of Andy Roxburgh and Craig Brown and the media insight of Hugh MacDonald and Jock Brown, to the ten fans who were lucky enough to go to Sweden – the fact they all took the time to assist is greatly appreciated. I extend further thanks to Craig for agreeing to write the foreword for the book; he is one of Scottish football's great characters and I am honoured that he has shared his memories in this story.

Thank you to Pitch Publishing for taking on the project when I first presented it to them last summer, in particular Jane Camillin. Her help and expertise have made life easier for me and I am grateful for the faith shown in me. Without the support of Pitch, this book may not have been possible.

Thank you to my family, close friends and everyone across social media for their messages of support when I first announced that I was writing the book. It means the world to me to know that so many of you were as excited about the idea as I was and I hope that I've done the story justice for you all. I'd also like to give a special mention to Neil Doherty, whose self-published book *World Cup 1998: Scotland's Story* gave me inspiration to attempt one of my own. For those who haven't read Neil's book, I highly recommend it.

Finally, a big thank you to my wonderful wife, Suzanne. Without her encouragement and support, I would not have taken this project on. You've been very patient when I've been stressed at certain times about this process, and I appreciate everything you've done for me during the seven months I've been working on the book. You may not like football but you recognise what it means to me, particularly following the Scotland national team, and for that I appreciate your support even more.

References

https://en.wikipedia.org/wiki/UEFA_Euro_1992

UEFA Euro 1992 qualifying – Wikipedia

UEFA Euro 1992 qualifying Group 2 – Wikipedia

https://anyflip.com/xsgz/yakw/ *Famous Tartan Army
Magazine* 2021 Issue 1 (Roxburgh interview)

https://anyflip.com/xsgz/tvkn/ *Famous Tartan Army
Magazine* 2021 Issue 2 (Gallacher interview)

Famous Tartan Army Magazine (anyflip.com)

Famous Tartan Army Magazine October 2020
(Brown interview)

https://www.scottishfa.co.uk/international-
matches/?mid=57534 Scotland v Romania

https://www.scottishfa.co.uk/international-
matches/?mid=57535 Scotland v Switzerland

https://www.scottishfa.co.uk/international-
matches/?mid=57536 Bulgaria v Scotland

https://www.scottishfa.co.uk/international-
matches/?mid=57538 Scotland v Bulgaria

https://www.scottishfa.co.uk/international-matches/?mid=57497 San Marino v Scotland

https://www.scottishfa.co.uk/international-matches/?mid=57498 Switzerland v Scotland

https://www.scottishfa.co.uk/international-matches/?mid=57499 Romania v Scotland

https://www.scottishfa.co.uk/international-matches/?mid=57500 Scotland v San Marino

https://www.scottishfa.co.uk/international-matches/?mid=57502 USA v Scotland

https://www.scottishfa.co.uk/international-matches/?mid=57503 Canada v Scotland

https://www.youtube.com/watch?v= – B55ctGfus Bulgaria v Romania

https://www.youtube.com/watch?v=SWiZ4V7nS9s Roy Aitken Official Scotland Podcast

Craig Brown and Bernard Bale, *The Game of My Life* (John Blacke Publishing 2001)

Pat Nevin *The Accidental Footballer* (Monoray Publishing 2021)

https://www.scottishfootballforums.co.uk/2021/09/s11e14-guest-special-stewart-mckimmie/

https://www.scottishfootballforums.co.uk/2021/08/s11e5-guest-special-dave-mcpherson/

https://www.scottishfootballforums.co.uk/2020/10/s10e14-robert-connor-interview/

https://www.scottishfootballforums.co.uk/2020/04/s9e42a-brian-irvine-interview-part-1/

Glasgow Herald articles dated 04/09/1990, 10/09/1990

https://www.worldometers.info/world-population/
san-marino-population/

https://www.czechuniversities.com/article/a-brief-
history-of-the-czech-republic

https://omniatlas.com/maps/europe/19920622/

https://www.11v11.com/matches/bulgaria-v-romania-
20-november-1991-243309/

https://thesetpieces.com/latest-posts/
choccys-diary-euros-adventures-scotland-
tournament-near-misses/

https://en.wikipedia.org/wiki/Yugoslav_Wars

https://podcasts.apple.com/us/podcast/
episode-43-interview-brian-mcclair-part-2/
id1250340626?i=1000466496246

https://www.youtube.com/watch?v=HM8sE3OiqNo
Scotland v Germany highlights

https://www.uefa.com/uefaeuro/match/5095 –
scotland-vs-germany/

https://www.uefa.com/uefaeuro-2020/news/0253-
0d7b30adf9ec-af42087d895e-1000 – bergkamp-
strikes-as-netherlands-edge-out-scotland-
in-euro-1992-/

https://www.uefa.com/uefaeuro-2020/news/0253-
0d7b30a36956-ffff29100847-1000 – scotland-take-
the-cis-down-with-them-in-euro-1992-group-1/

https://www.scottishfa.co.uk/international-
matches/?mid=57537 Scotland v USSR

https://www.youtube.com/watch?v=VCGS5aqR2oo
Bulgaria v Scotland

https://www.citypopulation.de/en/sweden/
admin/%C3%B6sterg%C3%B6tland/0581__
norrk%C3%B6ping/

https://theworld.org/stories/2015-12-28/half-million-
kids-survived-romanias-slaughterhouses-souls-
now-they-want-justice

https://www.youtube.com/watch?v=InKcjTLryMc
Rangers v Dundee United 1991, team lines at 0:06
proof Richard Gough missed the game (Chapter 3)

https://www.uefa.com/uefaeuro-2020/news/0253-
0d7bc692c194-ce0e0f567c1e-1000 – euro-1992-
team-of-the-tournament/

John Robertson *Robbo: My autobiography* (Black and
White Publishing, 2021)

1990 (September 12) Scotland – Romania (EC-1992
Qualifier). Full Game (part 1 of 4). – YouTube

1990 (September 12) Scotland – Romania (EC-1992
Qualifier). Full Game (part 2 of 4). – YouTube

1990 (September 12) Scotland – Romania (EC-1992
Qualifier). Full Game (part 3 of 4). – YouTube

1990 (September 12) Scotland – Romania (EC-1992
Qualifier). Full Game (part 4 of 4). – YouTube

Romania – Scotia ECQ 92, 16 oct 1991 – YouTube

Switzerland v Scotland European Championship
Qualifier 1991 (Full Match) – YouTube

1992 UEFA Euro (Qualifier) – Scotland vs
Switzerland. Full Match (Part 1 of 4). – YouTube

1992 UEFA Euro (Qualifier) – Scotland vs
Switzerland. Full Match (Part 2 of 4). – YouTube

1992 UEFA Euro (Qualifier) – Scotland vs
Switzerland. Full Match (Part 3 of 4). – YouTube
1992 UEFA Euro (Qualifier) – Scotland vs
Switzerland. Full Match (Part 4 of 4). – YouTube
Scotland Bulgaria 1991 1:1 – YouTube
1991 (May 1) San Marino 0-Scotland 2 (EC
Qualifier).mpg – YouTube
Scotland v San Marino 1992 European
Championship Qualifier – YouTube
scotland n ireland 92 part1 – YouTube
scotland n ireland 92 part2 – YouTube
1992 (march 25) Scotland 1-Finland 1 (Friendly).
avi – YouTube

Also available at all good book stores

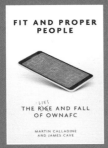

9781801500470

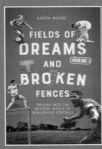

9781801501002

9781801500586

9781785314391

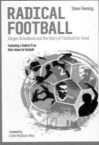

9781801501149

9781785311802

9781801500968

9781801500975

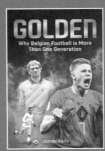

9781801501057